"This book is a must-have for any health professional working with patients who suffer from panic. Sandra Scheinbaum deals sensitively and authoritatively with the subject, presenting an effective, tried-and-tested functional approach that encourages the wellness of the body and the mind through positive thinking, diet, and exercise. It is a comprehensive resource that will help practitioners support their clients and incite genuine, sustainable transformation. I highly recommend this book!"

—*Dr. Mark Hyman, founder and medical director of The UltraWellness Center, chairman of the Institute for Functional Medicine and author of the #1 New York Times bestseller,* The Blood Sugar Solution

"Sandra Scheinbaum's book, *How to Give Clients the Skills to Stop Panic Attacks: Don't Forget to Breathe*, is a masterfully crafted guide to help those suffering from panic disorders. This splendid book integrates natural self-healing techniques that are safe and effective. You will find a new doorway to relaxation and self-control naturally!"

—*Gerard E. Mullin, Associate Professor of Medicine, The Johns Hopkins School of Medicine, Baltimore*

"The best person to write a book about panic attacks is someone who has overcome panic and anxiety in themselves and is now a health psychologist working with clients going through the same condition. That's what you have here in your hand. Sandra takes an integrative approach, blending together a gentle medical analysis of the condition with practical approaches for working with clients using both body and mind techniques. Presented with empathy, written from the heart, and a must-have for any wellness professional's bookshelf."

—*Laurel Alexander, complementary therapist, wellness coach and author of* How to Incorporate Wellness Coaching into Your Therapeutic Practice, *Sussex, UK*

of related interest

Make Yourself Better
A Practical Guide to Restoring Your Body's Wellbeing
Philip Weeks
ISBN 978 1 84819 012 1
eISBN 978 0 85701 077 3

Breaking Free From Persistent Fatigue
Lucie Montpetit
ISBN 978 1 84819 101 3

How to Incorporate Wellness Coaching into Your Therapeutic Practice
A Handbook for Therapists and Counsellors
Laurel Alexander
ISBN 978 1 84819 063 4
eISBN 978 0 85701 034 6

Seated Tai Chi and Qigong
Guided Therapeutic Exercises to Manage Stress and Balance Mind, Body and Spirit
Cynthia W. Quarta
ISBN 978 1 84819 088 7
eISBN 978 0 85701 071 1

Chair Yoga
Seated Exercises for Health and Wellbeing
Edeltraud Rohnfeld
Illustrated by Edeltraud Rohnfeld
Translated by Anne Oppenheimer
ISBN 978 1 84819 078 8
eISBN 978 0 85701 056 8

Meditation and Movement
Structured Therapeutic Activity Sessions
G. Rosser
ISBN 978 1 84905 018 0
eISBN 978 1 84642 944 6

Breath in Action
The Art of Breath in Vocal and Holistic Practice
Edited by Jane Boston and Rena Cook
ISBN 978 1 84310 942 6
eISBN 978 1 84642 948 4

Frog's Breathtaking Speech
How Children (and Frogs) Can Use the Breath to Deal with Anxiety, Anger and Tension
Michael Chissick
Illustrated by Sarah Peacock
ISBN 978 1 84819 091 7
eISBN 978 0 85701 074 2

How to Give Clients the Skills

to Stop Panic Attacks

Don't Forget to Breathe

Sandra Scheinbaum

Jessica Kingsley *Publishers*
London and Philadelphia

First published in 2012
by Jessica Kingsley Publishers
116 Pentonville Road
London N1 9JB, UK
and
400 Market Street, Suite 400
Philadelphia, PA 19106, USA

www.jkp.com

Library of Congress Cataloging in Publication Data
Scheinbaum, Sandra.
Don't forget to breathe : a guide to stopping panic attacks / Sandra Scheinbaum.
p. ; cm.
Includes bibliographical references.
ISBN 978-1-84905-887-2 (alk. paper)
I. Title.
[DNLM: 1. Panic Disorder--therapy. 2. Relaxation Therapy--methods. 3. Respiration. WM 172]

616.85'223--dc23
2011047782

British Library Cataloguing in Publication Data
A CIP catalogue record for this book is available from the British Library

ISBN 978 1 84905 887 2
eISBN 978 0 85700 603 5

Printed and bound in Great Britain

To my late mom, Faye Pecken,
who told herself every morning
that "it's going to be a good day."

Contents

Introduction

"Tension is who you think you are,
relaxation is who you are."
—Chinese Proverb

Panic and fear may appear to rule your life, but rather than being consumed by anxiety, imagine enjoying a state of inner quiet. Learn to calm your mind and body and stop anxious feelings from escalating into panic. You can recover from a full-blown panic attack. What's more, the positive steps you take create permanent neurological changes so panic episodes will be a distant memory.

Do you know someone who suffers from panic? Are you a therapist, coach or counselor who works with someone who suffers from panic? If so, effective treatment begins when you strongly convey the above message of hope. By engaging in a partnership to quiet the panic response, both trainer and trainee will find relaxation.

You can stop panic and anxiety.

By conveying this message, you're empowering your clients— communicating to them that they're in control and can change. But just mouthing the words won't create a therapeutic alliance. Consider also the disconnect that arises if you're having difficulty managing stress or struggling with your own anxieties and haven't been able to find inner peace. What works for me is the telling of my personal story.

About 35 years ago, I overcame panic and anxiety without the use of medication or traditional psychotherapy. Prior to that time, I jokingly referred to myself as a "nervous wreck." The worst period was in my early twenties when I developed debilitating panic attacks, which would spring up without any warning. One episode is particularly memorable:

My husband and I were spending the first winter in our new home in a Chicago suburb. One morning we awoke to discover three feet of snow outside. My husband left for work very early, but I stayed home due to a "snow day" at the school where I was teaching. The snow fell all morning and into the afternoon. I began worrying about being snowed in and decided to shovel the driveway. This was an activity that I didn't engage in on a regular basis. In fact, having grown up in an apartment building, I was a complete novice. Although the snow was quite deep, I made slow, steady progress down our long driveway. About midway, I decided to go into the house to warm up. That was when it happened.

As I removed my mittens, I couldn't catch my breath. When I took off my heavy coat, I noticed a feeling of light-headedness. I thought about the warnings regarding the dangers of shoveling snow. Breathing became more labored. I thought about how people have heart attacks due to shoveling snow. Then I observed that my left arm seemed numb. My thoughts turned to the memory of a pediatrician informing my mother that I had a heart murmur when I was five years old. I immediately felt chest pain. I was having a heart attack! What if I passed out? The shortness of breath and chest pains worsened. Incredible as it seemed, I was dying from a heart attack at 25 years old. Time to call 911.

The terrifying chain reaction occurred within two to three minutes. I called my husband and informed him of the seriousness of my condition. Although he was 20 miles away in downtown Chicago in the middle of a snowstorm, he rushed home.

When the paramedics arrived, the accompanying sights and sounds sent my heart rate through the roof. Visions of dying increased. Soon I arrived in the emergency room by stretcher. An EKG ruled out any evidence of a heart attack or cardiac abnormalities. Immediately, the chest pains disappeared. I began to relax as I was handed a paper bag and told to breathe into it. By that time, my frantic husband arrived expecting to find his wife in critical condition. I felt embarrassed and silly. Within a few minutes I was joking about the incident and feeling much better.

My fearful thoughts about the dangers of shoveling snow led to a classic panic attack. This was one of many such occurrences: walking down a busy street while on vacation, I suddenly felt dizzy and short of breath from cardiac exertion; sitting in a theatre watching a play, I noticed chest pains and worried about having to leave during the show and disrupt the audience; leaving an aerobics class as a new convert to exercise, I couldn't breathe and drove halfway to the emergency room before coming to my senses. Each of these episodes was caused by fearful thoughts, but I didn't know it at the time.

Still worried about the presence of a heart condition, I went to my internist and told him about the palpitations and difficulty breathing. I received a clean bill of health and a prescription for a drug called Inderal to help relax. Before taking the first pill, I read the label. A beta-blocker, this medication is used to treat angina, high blood pressure and heart rhythm disorders. Why was I given a drug for heart patients? The thought of taking it brought up all my fears about having heart disease. So I made the decision to find a better way to calm down and tossed the pills.

Around that time I began a doctoral program in clinical psychology and enrolled in a workshop about self-regulation therapies. On the first day of class, we were introduced to slow abdominal breathing and led through a relaxation practice. I was hooked! That was 36 years ago and I have not had a major panic attack since.

Since my doctoral training, I've studied integrative and functional medicine, nutrition, yoga, and cognitive-behavior therapy, collecting a variety of techniques for achieving inner peace. For over 30 years, I've taught these strategies to hundreds of patients in my private practice as a health psychologist. Good nutrition and breathing provide the foundation, positive images plus rational thoughts are the building blocks, and adding laughter, physical movement and meaningful activities supplies the finishing touches for staying panic-free. Every day, I find ways to integrate these basic processes into my life. That's why I can now shovel a driveway full of snow, and the thought of passing out or having a heart attack never crosses my mind.

> Picture yourself as calm and relaxed.
> Picture someone else panic-free.

I stopped having panic attacks because I applied mind–body therapies, including changing my diet and starting a physical exercise program. These approaches weren't taught in psychology departments at the time. I remember describing my panic episodes to a supervising psychologist, and he recommended four to five days a week of psychoanalysis.

When I trained to become a clinical psychologist in the early 1980s, most therapists subscribed to the psychodynamic school of thought. When I endorsed cognitive-behavior therapy, I was venturing into less well-charted territory; to go out on a limb and believe in a mind–body therapy was considered downright radical. The practice of psychology at the time was focused on treating the mind. Although it was acknowledged that the mind influences the body, how the body influences the mind wasn't considered. We weren't trained in nutrition and didn't study the benefits of physical movement. Although we've made some progress, by and large, little has changed. For example, the initial assessment forms favored by insurance companies who reimburse for mental health services have no questions about diet or exercise habits.

I strongly believe that we need a new practice model for treating and preventing mental health disorders, including panic and anxiety. That model is functional medicine, which incorporates an integrative approach to healthcare. Functional medicine is based on systems biology and takes into account the complex interactions of multiple organ systems and biochemical pathways with environmental and genetic influences.

According to the website of the Arizona Center for Integrative Medicine, integrative medicine is:

> healing-oriented medicine that takes account of the whole person (mind, body, and spirit), including all aspects of lifestyle. It emphasizes the therapeutic relationship and makes use of all appropriate therapies, both conventional and alternative. (www.integrativemedicine.arizona.edu)

The biomedical model of mental illness focuses on diagnosing and treating specific conditions with specific drugs or therapies, but is failing because lifestyle factors are largely ignored. All too often the conventional approach relies upon a one-size-fits-all mentality. An integrative mental health approach based on functional medicine focuses on each patient as an individual with unique biochemical, genetic, social, psychological, and energetic features. Rather than treating the disease, functional medicine treats the person who has the disease. Using this model, treating panic disorder doesn't mean matching symptoms to the name "panic" as outlined in the latest version of the *Diagnostic and Statistical Manual of Mental Disorders* (American Psychiatric Association 2000) and then applying whatever happens to be the current standard of care, which today is typically a combination of medication and cognitive-behavior therapy. Although I'm definitely in favor of learning to recognize and change irrational thought patterns, cognitive-behavior therapy focuses on the thinking brain. A holistic approach looks at the whole person: mind, body, and soul.

When using an integrative model rooted in functional medicine, the practitioner investigates the links between anxiety and other physical symptoms, such as fatigue, gastrointestinal distress, and abdominal obesity. The possibility of a common thread, such as systemic inflammation and oxidative stress, would be acknowledged and nutrition and lifestyle changes incorporated in a comprehensive treatment plan. Integrative mental health draws upon the collaborative efforts of a variety of health professionals and encompasses both Western and non-Western healing traditions.

In the following chapters, you'll learn a model for understanding panic based on functional medicine and find simple techniques for relaxing both mind and body. You'll discover the power of breathing merged with positive imagery and rational thinking, in addition to physical release through movement, body awareness, yoga postures, and even belly laughter. We'll explore the benefits of calming foods and supplements, and reducing toxic load. Finally, we'll discuss the role of medication.

Some of the methods described have not yet been validated by scientific research as treatments for anxiety. However, many have been successfully used for centuries in India and China. I've drawn upon the wisdom of other integrative health practitioners and have powerful anecdotal evidence from hundreds of patients I've seen personally that this approach works.

Functional medicine is an exciting model that is emerging as one of the most powerful trends in 21st-century healthcare. Rather than sticking with the traditional route of naming the disorder and then applying the treatment/medication to treat the condition, functional medicine involves a paradigm shift: listening to each client's story, then engaging in a partnership to create healing. The presenting complaint might be panic attacks, but by learning to breathe, use creative imagination, think rationally, and incorporate diet and lifestyle change, not only will the panic disappear, but other health issues will improve as well. These include depression, headaches, insomnia, gastrointestinal distress, high cholesterol, and even chronic medical conditions such as diabetes, heart disease, and cancer.

Creating a partnership for positive change isn't a one-way street. Both parties are active participants. As you read the following chapters use the italicized sections as potential scripts for helping others but also turn inward and use them for yourself. Consider the famous adage: "Physician, heal thyself." Apply the healing principles to your own life; practice the relaxation techniques yourself before teaching them to others. Write you own personal prescription for enjoyable exercise. Experiment with the food and supplement recommendations discussed in Chapter 9 and notice how you feel.

Incorporating these strategies into your life and professional practice should be enjoyable. Your role is not to change someone else. That's hard work and accomplishes nothing except activating your own stress response. Given support, encouragement and the right tools, healthy growth will take place and negative patterns will diminish. Most importantly, let go of any perceived need for maintaining a serious state of being. That doesn't help alleviate anxiety. I didn't use a scholarly tone when writing this book because I want you to have fun as you explore the many facets of stopping panic.

CHAPTER 1

Could This Be Panic?

Racing heart

Sweating

Trembling or shaking all over

Feeling as if you're going to faint

Difficulty catching your breath

Numbness or tingling up your arms and legs

Chest pains

Dry mouth

Nausea or abdominal discomfort

Clammy hands

Hot flashes or feelings of extreme coldness

Choking sensation

Weakness

Muscle aches or overall physical tension

Chest pains

Jitteriness

Feeling as if you have a "caffeine high" even though you didn't drink any coffee

Difficulty concentrating

Feeling as if everything is unreal or "out of body"

Ringing in the ears

Feeling dizzy or light-headed

Shakiness in your arms or legs

Feeling as if you can't walk

Feeling as if you're "going crazy"

Feeling as if you're dying

Do you know someone who describes the rapid onset of at least four of these symptoms? If so, then panic disorder would be the correct label. So now what? Attaching a name to a cluster of symptoms is usually considered the first step on the journey towards wellness. But finding the right label is only part of the story. In this chapter, we'll explore the process of coming to the diagnosis, identifying underlying causes, and presenting an integrative treatment plan.

Avoid Getting Stuck in a Medical Maze

The significance of that first communication with a healthcare professional about any of the above symptoms can't be overestimated. Because panic is often misdiagnosed or missed altogether by physicians, it's easy to get steered in the wrong direction, passed along from one specialist to another, and end up with the wrong label and/or treatment plan. Panic disorder in children may be overlooked entirely or misdiagnosed as another condition, such as attention deficit or oppositional-defiant disorder.

As heavy users of medical services, clients with panic disorder typically undergo extensive and costly diagnostic testing, the process itself often reinforcing the scary notion that they're suffering from some serious medical condition. Navigating through the medical system may take on a life of its own—one that's filled with opportunities for panicking. Many get stuck in this maze, because they're referred to more and more physicians when test after test yields negative findings. It's not uncommon to get referred to cardiologists, gastroenterologists, pulmonary specialists, rheumatologists, endocrinologists, neurologists, psychiatrists, and psychologists.

Also navigating their way through the medical maze are those who enter it voluntarily, because the label, "panic disorder" doesn't seem quite right. Given that the symptoms associated with panic are physical, it's hard to be convinced that a medical illness isn't present. Clinging to the belief that something must be physically wrong despite objective findings to the contrary, these individuals proceed from one doctor to the next, hoping for a definitive diagnosis of a medical condition. I've seen clients who've even made appointments with two or three physicians within a particular specialty, hoping that someone will tell them they have a serious malady.

Don't Ignore the Physical Body:
It May Not Be "All in Their Heads"

A functional medicine model takes into account physical reasons for panic. Factors such as digestive issues, lack of sleep, an overactive thyroid, poor diet, or toxic overload, may be contributing to an anxious state. You may have diagnosed someone with panic based upon the criteria outlined in the *Diagnostic and Statistical Manual of Mental Disorders* (American Psychiatric Association 2000), but the anxiety could have multiple underlying biological causes.

Maybe your client's anxiety is linked to eating gluten, which contains significant amounts of glutamate, an excitotoxin that changes brain function and behavior, or maybe the culprit is coffee, sugar, or high levels of environmental toxins. Maybe they're wired and exhausted and the panic attacks are part of a larger issue referred to as adrenal dysfunction. Maybe the root cause is a B12 deficiency or dehydration.

Have you considered spring or summer seasonal affective disorder (SAD), chronic fatigue, sleep apnea, premenstrual syndrome, binge eating, multiple chemical sensitivities, or the possibility of a systemic yeast infection? Is your client suffering from hyperthyroidism, chronic sinusitis, orthostatic hypotension (a sudden drop in blood pressure upon rising too quickly), Ménière's disease (an inner ear disorder affecting balance), Addison's disease (adrenal insufficiency), diabetes, or Lyme disease? Mitral valve prolapse, a benign condition in which the heart's mitral valve doesn't close tightly, has also been linked to panic.

Move Beyond Attaching the Right Name

Finally, the frustrating search for answers comes to an end. Serious medical conditions have been ruled out and underlying biological factors associated with panic may or may not have been identified. Either way, let's assume that both physician and patient cast their vote and panic disorder is the winning diagnosis. Unfortunately, what follows might be a discussion about panic as a mental health disorder, ending with patients inevitably handed a prescription for an anti-anxiety drug. They may leave thinking it's "all in my head" and subscribe to the theory that panic is a mental illness.

Mental health professionals unwittingly harm their clients by reinforcing a disease model. Even if they don't prescribe medication, they may create another type of addiction: addiction to psychotherapy. I've even heard clients say that being in therapy for life was recommended. Describing panic as an illness reinforces fear.

Imagine how you would feel upon hearing the news that you don't have a serious medical condition and you're not mentally ill? Rather, it's just plain old panic. For many, after receiving the correct label, a huge weight lifts as they realize that they're not on the verge of dying or going crazy. I like to inform newly diagnosed clients that at least one quarter of the population suffers from anxiety at one time or another, and that panic is one of the most common reasons for going to the emergency room.

Start with Hope

Which patient will have a better outcome? Patient A goes to see her doctor because she's experiencing many of the symptoms described above and learns that she's suffering from panic disorder. The physician informs her that panic is hard to recover from and she'll probably need medication the rest of her life. Patient B experiences the same symptoms, gets the same diagnosis, but receives the hopeful message that he can learn to stop a panic attack, can accomplish this without medication or lengthy talk therapy, and that complete recovery is possible.

Having the correct label and learning that panic is extremely common can be comforting and possessing the knowledge that they're not sick and about to die can shorten the duration of a panic attack for many clients. But the journey towards wellbeing begins with an optimistic message. Don't respond like the well-meaning professionals who unwittingly reinforce the panic response by describing it as genetic (meaning nothing can be done about it), a mental illness (meaning it's not my fault, I have a handicapping disease), a life-long condition, or a disorder that's hard to treat without medication or long-term therapy.

Sometimes physicians say something to a patient with no history of panic and that message becomes the underlying trigger for future panic attacks. One of my clients recalled being told by his doctor that he may have a minor problem with his heart that didn't require further evaluation or medical attention. Full-blown panic disorder developed shortly thereafter. Would the outcome have been different if the message had been worded differently? When I was a child, I recall the pediatrician telling my mother that I had a heart murmur (later disproven). Memories of that conversation, plus a family history of heart disease were the powerful predisposing factors that led to my panic episodes.

The more positive the message delivered by health professionals, the greater the chances of both averting and recovering from panic. Rather than setting clients back before they begin, start with a hopeful theme: "Although these symptoms are very scary, the good news is that you can learn to stop a panic attack. I'll be your guide as we discover the best ways for you to quiet yourself."

Acknowledge any "Overlays"

At the beginning, the symptoms listed earlier just exist. But the mind immediately gets busy interpreting and judging, resulting in the inevitable progression to a higher level of panic. I refer to these fears as "overlays," or "panicking about panic." If you posed these questions to your clients, would any of the following sound familiar?

> *Are you afraid that panic will suddenly come over you, as if appearing out of nowhere?*
>
> *Do you worry about not being able to function?*
>
> *Are you embarrassed or ashamed of these feelings?*
>
> *Do you worry that you'll always feel this way?*
>
> *Are you asking yourself, "why me?"*
>
> *Do you worry about why is this happening?*
>
> *Do you think that you alone have these scary sensations?*
>
> *Do you think that you're going crazy?*
>
> *Are you afraid that you're mentally ill?*
>
> *Do you fear having to go to a psychiatrist, taking medication, or being put in a psychiatric hospital?*
>
> *Are you resorting to alcohol or drugs to "take the edge off"?*

Notice how the above questions pertain to new categories completely unrelated to the original physical sensations. Instead, they involve secondary fears: fear of embarrassment and shame, worries about loss of control or ability to function, and fear of going crazy. As a result, some may suffer in silence and wait years before seeking help. The longer the symptoms persist, the greater the likelihood that feelings of helplessness, hopelessness, and worthlessness develop. Now the original panic signs have an additional attachment: panic disorder with depression.

Many clients perceive themselves as helpless victims of panic with little control over their physical being. Because dreading loss of control is such a prominent overlay, panic attacks frequently occur in situations or locations that reinforce the sense of not being in control. Common high-risk settings include airplanes, the middle row of seats in an auditorium, or a car that's stuck in heavy traffic. The thought "I can't leave!" leads to the physical symptoms associated with panic.

Dreading the fear response, many find it hard to resist their doctor, family member, or friend who tells them that they need to be on medication. I've worked with many clients who've been scared into believing that they'll need to be on anti-anxiety drugs for the rest of their lives because they're afraid of experiencing the panic sensations. Parents are frequently pressured by teachers and pediatricians to place their child on medication. Some feel guilty if they resist this pressure, while others experience guilt about "drugging" their child or "taking the easy way out." Either way, a parental "overlay" increases anxiety for all concerned.

Ask about and acknowledge any or all of these "overlays" as perfectly normal as you continue to reinforce the hopeful message that generating a panic response is just a habit, like any other bad habit. That message might go something like this:

> *Yes, the sensations feel weird and scary right now, but you'll discover a better way of being by learning and practicing. Soon new habits will replace old ones.*

When working with children, I frequently begin by addressing parental anxieties, including their fears about their child's fears, emphasizing that anxiety can be a "communicable" condition within the family.

Move Forward from Retreats

It's rare to encounter clients who don't develop an "overlay" and then proceed to retreat and purposely avoid particular places or encounters. For example, they may:

- avoid highways
- avoid driving alone
- avoid driving over bridges or through tunnels
- avoid driving altogether
- stay away from shopping malls or large stores
- turn down social invitations
- stop going to the grocery store
- avoid sitting in the center of a row at the movies or in a theater
- avoid going to plays or movies altogether

- avoid sporting events
- take a seat near the exit
- avoid crowds
- stay away from restaurants
- avoid public speaking
- prefer staying at home
- fear exercising
- avoid going outside when it's very hot, very cold, or very windy
- fear feeling trapped
- fear being away from someone with whom they feel safe.

Here's a way to acknowledge retreating while emphasizing moving forward:

The first panic attack may have been so terrifying that you're afraid of having another one. If you're literally "afraid of being afraid," that's perfectly normal. Most people who suffer from anxiety progress to "fearing fear." The longer the symptoms are experienced, the more likely it is that you're panicking about the possibility of having a panic attack. What happens now? When you're anxious about being anxious, maybe you think twice before engaging in an activity or going to a particular place where you previously had a panic attack. You start retreating from these settings or worry about when a panic attack might occur. As a result, you end up feeling even more anxious. It may seem like your world is getting smaller and smaller, but we're going to work together so you can move forward.

Children with panic may retreat from routine activities such as going to school, engaging in extracurricular programs, taking field trips, socializing with friends, or sleeping away from home. In my experience, parents often scare themselves by thinking "my child will always be this way" or feel pressured by teachers, family, or friends to act quickly and "do something," thereby raising both their and their child's anxiety level.

Don't Forget about the Myths

Along with a hopeful message regarding recovery, it's important to address the myths surrounding panic. A panic episode may be frightening, but it's not dangerous. Use the following myth-busters as needed.

MYTH#1: PANIC CAN CAUSE A HEART ATTACK, HEART FAILURE, OR CARDIAC ARREST

If you have heart disease, an electrocardiogram (EKG) detects noticeable electrical changes. During a panic attack, your heart beats faster. That's all.

In *The Anxiety and Phobia Workbook*, Edmund Bourne (1990) suggests informing clients that the heart can withstand quite a lot, as it's made up of very strong and dense muscle fibers.

MYTH #2: PANIC LEADS TO CESSATION OF BREATHING OR SUFFOCATION

A panic attack will not cause you to stop breathing or suffocate. Under stress, chest and neck muscles tighten, which limits breathing capacity. But don't worry, the brain has a built-in reflex mechanism that forces you to breathe if you're not getting enough oxygen. You'll automatically gasp and take a deep breath long before reaching the point where you could pass out from a lack of oxygen. Even if you did pass out, you would immediately start breathing again.

MYTH #3: PANIC LEADS TO FAINTING

You may be feeling light-headed because blood circulation to the brain is reduced, but a panic attack won't cause you to faint.

MYTH #4: PANIC CAUSES LOSS OF BALANCE AND FALLS

A panic attack may cause you to feel dizzy because the stress response may be affecting the inner ear. But panic cannot cause you to lose your balance. I understand you feel "weak in the knees." That's because the adrenaline surging through your body causes blood to accumulate in your leg muscles. The good news is the legs don't lose strength, and you won't fall over or be unable to walk.

MYTH #5: PANIC MEANS I'M "GOING CRAZY"

You're breathing quickly during a panic attack, which reduces blood supply to the brain and causes constriction of blood vessels. The result: feeling disoriented. Although it certainly feels like an out-of-body experience, you can't "go crazy" during a panic attack or have what used to be referred to as a "nervous breakdown." In fact, you're perfectly capable of thinking and functioning normally because these sensations are meant to protect you. There's no evidence that psychotic conditions, such as schizophrenia, stem from panic attacks. We don't see visions, hear voices, or become delusional during a panic attack.

MYTH #6: PANIC LEADS TO LOSS OF CONTROL

A panic attack won't cause you to "lose control" or act in a bizarre way. You won't burst out screaming or harm yourself. It may seem as if you're "losing it," but the opposite occurs: all senses reach a heightened state of alertness in order to protect you.

This is a particularly important message to convey to adolescents, who are afraid they might embarrass themselves in front of their peers.

Emphasize the Confusing Nature of Panic

Expect the unexpected when dealing with panic attacks, as there's often no predictable pattern or consistency. Clients describe feeling perfectly fine one day but then have a major panic attack the following day at the same location. Often the rapid onset doesn't seem to make any sense.

Some convince themselves that it's not panic and must be something more serious, because the sensations seem to come "out of nowhere," even overtaking them when they're feeling good. In response, I tell them that this commonly heard scenario actually supports the diagnosis of panic. If panic attacks were based on reason, they would only occur in situations that were truly dangerous. We're *supposed* to be scared when faced with life-threatening emergencies. On the other hand, panic seems to develop out of the blue. By taking a closer look, there may be warning signs, such as elevations in heart rate or changes in breathing pattern leading up to the panic episode that supposedly appeared "out of nowhere."

The late Jerilyn Ross, founder of the Anxiety Disorders Association of America, and author of *Triumph over Fear: A Book of Help and Hope for People with Anxiety* (Ross 1994), panicked if she went above the tenth floor while living in New York. However, as an expert skier, she was perfectly relaxed on chair lifts. Her anxiety made no sense. My own experience also illustrates how arbitrary and nonsensical anxiety reactions can be. I have no fears of falling or injuring myself doing headstands and handstands as part of my yoga practice. However, get me near a downward moving escalator in an airport and I freak out at the thought of stepping on with heavy luggage trailing behind.

We're All in This Together

The symptoms now have a name, and you're forming a partnership to set off on a transformative journey towards health. Now's not the time to become a blank screen. Instead, reinforce the healing message that everyone has anxieties by sharing your own personal stories along with the coping tools and strategies that you find most helpful. When talking on the phone with potential clients referred because of anxiety, I disclose my history of panic attacks and reassure them that the feelings they're describing are ones I've experienced myself. I also mention that I recommend strategies I've either used or would consider using myself.

Group appointments also reinforce the theme that "you're not alone." Over the years, I've run diagnosis-specific groups because I believed that approach fostered a sense of community. Now, I'm less attached to the label when recommending group programs. Whether someone's been diagnosed with panic, generalized anxiety, depression, diabetes, obesity, cancer, heart disease, or an autoimmune condition, they all have fears and are coming together to heal the mind and body with breathing, food as medicine, and positive lifestyle changes.

Fostering a sense of community also develops from outside resources such as self-help books, websites, blogs, and chat rooms. With or without your endorsement, your clients are most likely seeking out these materials, so why not be proactive and suggest ones that will be particularly helpful? (See Appendix 1: Resources.)

For anyone struggling with accepting that their symptoms fall under the panic umbrella, recommending specific books or websites may be useful. In addition to the popular self-help guides, also suggest novels about people who overcame anxiety. These resources reinforce the message that panic is a common occurrence, help clients gain a better understanding of their problem, and reassure them that widely practiced effective solutions are within reach.

Assigning homework or suggesting reading materials might backfire if you're not completely familiar with and supportive of the material. Additionally, clients may be living with panic day and night and obsessing about their symptoms. The last thing they need is further immersion in "what's wrong" by reading about panic or doing homework assignments that they misinterpret. For these reasons, I typically don't recommend any self-help books pertaining to panic without providing specific guidance as to how to use and interpret the materials. As we get to know each other better, I may suggest specific chapters to reinforce what we've been focusing on. If clients ask for something to read during our initial visit, I suggest picking up any good novel that will "take them away" from the panic symptoms. I also recommend books that support the functional medicine and integrative approach that we'll be using. These include *The UltraMind Solution* by Dr. Mark Hyman (Hyman 2009), *Unstuck* by Dr. James Gordon (Gordon 2008: technically about healing from depression, but the approach works just as well for anxiety), Dr. Jon Kabat-Zinn's classic book *Full Catastrophe Living* (Kabat-Zinn 1990), and Dr. Andrew Weil's latest self-help book *Spontaneous Happiness* (Weil 2011).

An Integrative Model for Treating Panic

A functional medicine model removes the division between mind and body. The mind contributes to the health of the body, and the health of the body contributes to the health of the mind. Mental health professionals often take a narrow view by focusing extensively on past trauma or early childhood influences in order to uncover root causes. This approach only reinforces the problem by keeping clients stuck in their heads rehashing the past. Similarly, practitioners who believe that cognitive-behavior therapy is the best approach to stopping panic may also be employing reductionist thinking and missing the bigger picture. Clients are often frustrated and disappointed when they discover, sometimes after years of psychotherapy, that they can't talk their way out of panic.

Dr. Mark Hyman, in *The UltraMind Solution* (2009), makes the case that what happens in the body influences the brain. Nutritional deficiencies, food allergies and intolerances, toxins, and digestive, immune, hormonal and metabolic imbalances all impact brain health. Correcting these deficiencies and imbalances can dramatically improve brain functioning.

Conventional healthcare, including mental health services, generally asks two questions: What illness do you have and what drug and/or therapy method can be prescribed to treat it? Functional medicine asks the following questions: Why do you have these symptoms at this time, why are the mind and body out of balance, and how can we work together to find balance again? This integrative approach uses mind–body techniques, diet, and lifestyle changes as treatment modalities.

Panic can be successfully treated with functional medicine.

It's All about Balance

While explaining the integrative functional medicine model to clients, I talk a lot about balance:

> *Imagine a scale of justice with the heavy burden of panic and chronic stress weighing down one side while the other side, the relaxation response, holds the weight of a feather. The scale can tip in the other direction by lightening the load on one end, i.e., removing stressors, such as toxic thoughts and inflammatory foods, and increasing weight to the other side by adding quieting breaths, healing foods, good thoughts and images, and positive connections.*

Emphasize to clients that although panic attacks indicate a state of imbalance, coming into balance occurs on its own when the above changes take place. Again, picture a scale. Once weights are added to one side and/or subtracted from the other, the scale balances on its own.

> *Think about how everything in nature is in constant flux; nothing stays still. The same is true with the human body. Changes take place every second. Also consider a basic principle of physics: every action has an opposite and equal reaction. If we can produce one extreme, we're capable of producing the opposite reaction. Right now you're a master at being mindful of all the negative experiences you feel. With patience and practice, soon you'll become skilled at relaxing and be able to stop a panic attack with mindfulness of all that's positive.*

Dr. James Gordon, in *Unstuck* (2008), sees depression as an imbalance and a challenge, not a disease and a misfortune. I want clients to look at panic in the same way and become active participants in learning and healing, rather than viewing themselves as victims of a disease. Although they fear loss of control, they already have all the control they need but don't realize it yet. To make this point, consider using stories. The following classic works well, and not just with children:

> *Are you familiar with* The Wizard of Oz? *Remember how Dorothy was wearing the ruby slippers all along that would take her back to Kansas? You're wearing the ruby slippers right now: the relaxation side of the autonomic nervous system. In other words, you always had the power!*

In the next chapter, we'll take a closer look at the workings of the autonomic nervous system.

CHAPTER 2

What's Real in the Mind is Real in the Body

How Understanding Panic Leads to Stopping It

My favorite explanation of the panic response comes from an imaginary story told to me many years ago by Judith A. Green, Ph.D., one of the early pioneers in the field of biofeedback. Clients find it easy to follow and remember.

> *Pretend it's late at night and you're either driving or being driven home. All lights are out and you're surrounded by total darkness as you open the car door and step out. Suddenly you feel something around your ankle... It's a Snake!*

> *Imagine that moment. Gripped by fear, your heart pounds and you can't catch your breath. Maybe your stomach tightens into a knot. Maybe your arms and legs become numb. Maybe you begin to shake.*

> *Welcome to "fight or flight," our biological response to danger. To understand its purpose, go back in time and pretend you're walking through a forest thousands of years ago. Suddenly you notice a bear headed straight towards you. At that moment, you have only two choices: fight for your life or turn around and run for your life as fast as you can. Hence the term "fight or flight."*

> *To effectively fight or run away from imminent danger, you need blood supply to the appropriate muscle groups and internal organs. Your heart beats faster to accomplish this. Blood is drawn away from areas that aren't directly involved in fighting or running away and directed to*

more important places. For example, blood leaves your fingers and toes, the surface of your skin, and the parts of your brain that have to do with planning, reasoning and concentration. The last occurs because fighting or running away are reflex actions that don't require thinking or planning. Extremities may feel cold, numb or tingly when blood is shunted away.

Muscles brace in preparation for fighting. Sometimes they're tensing so hard they shake or tremble. The flight part of the fight-or-flight mechanism involves running. Running implies movement. Picture an animal that is caught but is struggling to break free. That's why pacing, finger or foot tapping, and the thought "I've got to get out of here" are common responses to anxiety.

Breathing speeds up to get more oxygen to the tissues involved in fighting or running away. You take quick gasps of breath through the upper chest because that's the fastest way to get oxygen. Because the chest muscles are working hard to do all this breathing, pain or tightness may be experienced. Dizziness, light-headedness, and feelings of unreality are also connected to this increased rate of breathing.

Both vision and hearing become sharper to better detect danger. You may break out into a sweat because the body knows that you're working hard while fighting or running away and it's important to stay cool. But you may also feel hot from all that exertion. The adrenal glands are working overtime to secrete a sufficient amount of stress hormones to drive the whole process.

Every organ in your body engages in the fight-or-flight response. Some are directly involved with the battle, while others are in a holding pattern so that all resources can be directed to the emergency. Which systems are put on hold? It's not important to digest your food when a predator is approaching, as all your energy must go towards fighting or running away. Therefore, digestion is put on hold, even at the level of saliva production. Similarly, your immune system is compromised because its work isn't required in the current battle.

The sympathetic branch of the autonomic nervous system prepares the body to fight or run away. Originating in the brain, sympathetic projections exit the spine and branch out to almost every organ, blood vessel and sweat gland. They even project to the thousands of tiny little hairs on the body. In a state of sheer terror, these hairs literally "stand on end." Have you ever heard someone who was frightened say, "That gave me goose bumps?" This temporary skin condition results from contraction of the tiny muscles that elevate the hair follicles.

For a more in-depth discussion of the fight-or-flight response, Robert Sapolsky's *Why Zebras Don't Get Ulcers* (2004) is a great read. The work of Shelley Taylor, Ph.D. at the University of California, Los Angeles may also be of interest, as she suggests that the physiology of the stress response may be different in women. Under stress, men fight or flee, but women may tend and befriend, preferring to take care of loved ones and talk to friends. The alarm response is about preparing the body for a big expenditure of energy, but females are typically less aggressive than males and having young children may rule out flight as an option (Taylor *et al.* 2000). It should be noted that this theory may pertain more to chronic sympathetic arousal as opposed to the sudden and intense activation of the alarm response that causes a panic attack.

Just a Garden Hose

Now let's go back to the snake coiled around your leg. Imagine the car door opening a little more so that the interior light comes on. You look down and realize that you stepped on a garden hose.

The emergency has passed. Seeing a garden hose is the same as sensing that the bear has moved off in another direction. Gradually, you breathe easily again and your heart rate slows down. The stomach returns to digesting food, the immune system resumes its maintenance work and blood flows back to your hands and feet as well as the brain centers responsible for problem solving.

The parasympathetic branch of the autonomic nervous system now takes over. Besides inducing calmness, it promotes energy storage and growth. While the sympathetic response tells the heart to beat faster, the parasympathetic response slows it down. Rather than sending blood to the muscles, the parasympathetic branch sends blood to the extremities. The sympathetic branch inhibits digestion, but the parasympathetic response stimulates digestion. The sympathetic and parasympathetic divisions can't operate at the same time. That would be like putting your foot on the gas and the brake simultaneously. It's either one or the other. You're either stepping on the gas or the brake. There's no in-between. The parts of the brain that activate one branch inhibit the other.

Here's the Crucial Question

If it was just a garden hose all along and not a snake, what was responsible for triggering the fight-or-flight response?

The word/mental image "Snake."

What was responsible for stopping the fight-or-flight response?

The word/mental image "Garden hose."

Consider every thought, every mental image and every word you say to yourself, as a shower of messages generated in the higher levels of the cerebral cortex, the parts of the brain that control language and thought processes.

Now imagine that all words that comprise our inner language and all mental images are sorted into two laundry bins: one for "darks" and one for "lights." There's no in-between. Every thought, image and word must go into one or the other.

Where did the word "snake" go? Because you associate snakes with danger, it went into the dark pile.

The conscious mind generates the association between the sensation of something coiled around your ankle and the image/word "snake."

The lower brainstem sorts the images and words into darks or lights. Once a danger signal is detected, the cascade of physiological changes takes place, including changes in the levels of circulating hormones. Cortisol, 17-hydroxy-corticosteroids, and the catecholamines, epinephrine, and norepinephrine, are elevated. Levels of growth hormones, glucose, prolactin, cholesterol, and uric acid increase as well. Adrenaline, a hormone secreted by the adrenal glands, activates the sympathetic nervous system.

Imagine walking around with a built-in alarm system, a home alarm device that's armed and ready to go off 24 hours a day. When a particular thought or mental image is sorted into the danger pile, you've put your finger on the home alarm button, signaling an emergency and the siren blares.

A Crucial Point to Remember

An emergency response team must work quickly. The bear is coming towards you and there's no time to lose. Therefore, the fight-or-flight response operates as quickly as a reflex, as fast as the reaction that takes place when you accidentally touch a hot stove.

It's easy to forget this important point in the midst of a scary panic attack. Here's a common scenario: Someone feels panicky so they take a breath because someone told them breathing helps, but they notice that they're still feeling their heart pounding or their knees about to buckle. They proceed to tell themselves that breathing isn't working. Maybe they attempt to distract themselves by turning on the TV or listening to music, but they inevitably check in with how they're feeling, and the panicky feelings still exist. Therefore, they conclude that breathing doesn't work and neither does distraction. What's wrong with this picture?

In the throes of panic, they forgot that panic, because it's actually the fight-or-flight survival response, develops within seconds, while the relaxation response takes time to kick in.

Imagine walking into a room and flipping a light switch. The room instantly lights up. That's the panic response; the sudden surge of adrenaline. The relaxation response resembles going from room to room turning off each individual lamp separately. Think of that process as the time it takes for the adrenaline to be reabsorbed into the body and all systems to get the "all clear" signal.

The more knowledge clients have about the workings of the sympathetic and parasympathetic branches of the autonomic nervous system, the easier it becomes for them to wait patiently until the panic sensations subside. One of my favorite analogies comes from a client: she imagines the panic episode as a long freight train passing by. Initially she hears intense rumbling as she watches the moving cars, but eventually she sees the caboose, the train disappears into the distance and the roar softens until silence again fills the air.

Panic sufferers frequently tell me that their attacks "come out of nowhere." They may be walking down the street or standing in line at the supermarket and the panic just hits them. This assumption that panic just "hits you out of the blue" stems from the lightning-quick speed of a reflex. But by dissecting the process to find the panic-producing thought or mental image, the cycle becomes clear.

We know that thoughts and images create changes at a physical level. For example, saliva production increases when we think about or smell food. If we think that something awful is going to happen, the entire body responds.

What's real in the mind is real in the body. The autonomic nervous system doesn't differentiate between past, present, and future.

Whenever we generate a thought or mental image, the autonomic nervous system responds as if it were an actual event in the present. The stronger the emotional response to a particular thought or image, the greater the intensity of the body's involvement.

For example, if while reading this paragraph you suddenly think about getting up for a snack, your body would be programming itself to perform the action. But since you're not emotionally attached to getting some food, very little energy would be invested in that programming. As a result, although the thought would create very subtle changes in breathing and brain wave patterns, there would be little change in the physical body. If you were to consider getting up for a snack but start to worry about caloric intake or whether you really need to eat right now, this emotional reaction would be sorted into the "dark" pile and a tiny bit of arousal would be stirred up. However, if you were to think about feeling short of breath or nauseous, these thoughts would be the "snakes" that trigger the alarm system, and a considerable amount of arousal would be generated in the physical body.

For a panic reaction to develop, a negative feedback loop must be created between mind and body. Each influences and reacts to the other in an escalating pattern of arousal. For example, you notice physical tension, so you say to yourself: "I must be getting anxious." The body then reacts to this "danger" thought by becoming more aroused. In other words, you've activated the sympathetic alarm system. Now you notice your heart rate increasing and think: "I'm going to have a panic attack!" The body has now received an even stronger signal to sound the alarm and prepare for danger ahead.

What was the "snake" when I had a severe panic attack while shoveling snow?

The snake was the idea that shoveling snow can cause a heart attack. If I had recognized that the sensations I was experiencing were panic and had known that a panic attack can't cause a heart attack, I would have turned off the alarm response.

Summing It All Up

Saying the word "snake" or having a mental picture of a snake is equivalent to pressing the emergency button on an alarm system. The alarm system doesn't know that it's a false alarm, so it directs the body's survival mechanism to gear up for fighting or running away.

The body mobilizes for the threat in a split second, so it's often hard to see the connection between thoughts or images and the body's responses to them. You think you're actually sick and are scared by these physical sensations.

Maybe you try to breathe or distract yourself, but the symptoms continue because the panic response can only be replaced by the relaxation response in a very slow fashion.

One thought, such as "breathing isn't working… I'm still feeling anxious," is sorted by the brain as a negative, "danger" thought. Thus the cycle continues and you still feel panicky.

Very simply, here's the key to stopping panic attacks:

Turn snakes into garden hoses and engage the safety mechanism rather than setting off the home alarm.

These two processes, when engaged in simultaneously, represent the essence of all mind–body therapies. Change your negative thoughts and images, and at the same time relax your body.

Pair negative thinking and scary images with constricted chest breathing and the fight-or-flight response turns on. Do so when you are sleep-deprived, haven't exercised, have consumed several cups of coffee or overindulged in a sugary snack, and it's even easier to get worked up to a panicky state. Pair realistic thinking and soothing images with slow, abdominal breathing, and the alarm system gets the message to turn off. Get an adequate amount of rest, remove what may be harmful, such as caffeine, sugar, and environmental toxins, feed your body the right nutrients, exercise, find laughter and meaningful connections, and the relaxation response strengthens. When the parasympathetic branch of the autonomic nervous system emerges as a strong counterbalance to sympathetic arousal, positive physical changes take place, even on a cellular level. With practice, these changes become permanent, so that the fight-or-flight response is only triggered during true emergencies.

In the following chapters, I'll explain how to change snakes into garden hoses, and how to find the safety mechanisms that turn off the alarm system.

CHAPTER 3

Don't Forget To Breathe
Building the Foundation of Relaxation

"Breath is the horse; mind is the rider."
—Ancient Tibetan Buddhist Saying

- "All I have to do to stop a panic attack is remember to breathe."

- "Whenever I feel as if I need to leave a crowded room, I go into my relaxed breathing and feel better."

- "I was about to panic when driving on the highway, but then I slowed down my breathing and the panicky feelings went away."

- "The thought of passing out crossed my mind, but I remembered your breathing techniques and the fear went away."

- "I was afraid that I would have a panic attack during my speech but slowed down my breathing and knew I'd be okay."

- "Seated in the middle of the row in a theater, I noticed the familiar sensation of my heart pounding, as I imagined having a panic attack and not being able to leave during the performance. Then I remembered to practice the breathing and began calming myself down. I even enjoyed the play!"

Over the years, I've heard similar comments from hundreds of patients. They repeatedly report that the key to stopping a panic attack is remembering to breathe. After becoming aware of my own dysfunctional breathing pattern, I focused on changing it. As a result, my panic attacks stopped.

Dr. Andrew Weil, a renowned pioneer in the field of integrative medicine, stated at a conference that I attended: "If I had to limit my advice on healthier living to just one tip, it would be simply to learn how to breathe properly." Because breathing profoundly affects the chemistry and function of the nervous system, it's the body's best way of healing itself. Dr. Weil's two-CD set, which provides an easy-to-follow course of eight breathing exercises, is entitled *Breathing: The Master Key to Self Healing* (see Appendix 1: Resources).

I also had the privilege of studying with Dr. James Gordon, Director of the Center for Mind–Body Medicine in Washington, D.C., who believes that slow belly breathing may be the single best anti-stress medicine that exists. It's so powerful that he teaches it to nearly every patient he sees.

During a panic attack, the mind races ahead to what might happen next, but breathing takes place in the present moment. Plus, the more the mind becomes occupied with focusing on the breath, the more it's distracted from the panic sensations. Occasionally, someone wants more information on the actual science behind the benefits of slow, deep breathing. Here's what we know:

The vagus nerve flows from the brain into the chest, and through the diaphragm. As the diaphragm expands while drawing in a belly breath, the vagus nerve is stimulated, and via the neurotransmitter acetylcholine, activates the parasympathetic response. Because this neurotransmitter is also involved in turning off the inflammatory response, relaxed breathing dials down inflammation.

You can also draw upon teachings that date back thousands of years to explain the benefits of relaxed breathing. Chinese medicine refers to *qi* or *chi* (pronounced chee) as the essential energy or vital life force. Inhalation draws in *qi* in addition to fresh oxygen. During exhalation, toxins and waste products are expelled. Similarly, the ancient yoga masters refer to *prana*, which in Sanskrit means "living or ultimate energy." We must breathe to maintain this powerful force that unites body and mind.

Having provided knowledge as to the importance of breathing, you're ready to take the next steps: recognizing dysfunctional breathing patterns, coaching relaxed breathing, and helping clients overcome the obstacles to maintaining a smooth, comfortable flow of breath.

A Dysfunctional Pattern and Panic Go Hand in Hand

When you are in the throes of panic, the scary sensations take center stage, so who can remember to breathe or trust the power of the breath? A perceived inability to breathe creates panic. In my case, the awareness that I couldn't catch my breath ignited the panic attacks, and hyperventilation quickly followed. Because breathing is associated with panic, many people believe that focusing on their breath will make them feel worse.

- "How can I focus on breathing when it feels as if I can't breathe?"
- "I tried your breathing techniques and felt light-headed, like I would pass out."
- "How do you expect me to remember that breathing thing when I'm in the middle of an activity or a conversation?"
- "The panic just comes over me before I can change my breathing."
- "I don't have time to think about breathing during the day."
- "If I think about how I'm breathing, I get upset and more panicky."
- "When I breathe the way you told me to, I don't get enough air."
- "When I breathe with my stomach, my stomach hurts."
- "Focusing on breathing makes my chest feel tight."
- "I'm working so hard to breathe the right way that I'm getting tense."
- "I can't walk around all day thinking about my breathing."
- "I'm too old to learn a new way of breathing."
- "When I practice breathing, I feel dizzy and light-headed."
- "I don't have the discipline to practice."
- "Focusing on breathing makes me feel worse."

I've heard these objections from patients in the initial phase of seeking help. Here's my response:

Of course you have negative thoughts and reactions to focusing on breathing. Nearly everyone suffering from panic feels uncomfortable and complains about not getting enough air. You're a beginning student learning a new skill. Remember when you first learned to read or ride a bike. It was difficult at first, and you made mistakes or felt awkward. But you didn't give up. You persisted and kept practicing. Gradually, it got easier and you mastered the technique. Learning relaxed breathing is easier than learning a completely new skill, because your body already knows what to do. That's because you were breathing in a natural way as a baby.

Tell clients that you're going to work together to find a breathing pattern that's right for them. Make sure they understand that they're not being told to take time out of their busy day to practice deep breathing. Provide reassurances that relaxed breathing won't turn them into unproductive zombies and won't lead to loss of control. We're aiming for alert, yet relaxed. To reinforce this concept, I might draw an inverted U-shaped curve with total relaxation on one end and extreme panic on the other. *You're going to experience the top of the curve, which is a great place to be throughout the day.* To illustrate that this state can be reached, I show them that I'm practicing a relaxed breathing style, even though I'm focused, alert, and speaking.

Use this chapter as a guide to coaching clients, but more importantly, use it as a personal guide for examining and modifying your own breathing style. Start by recognizing any dysfunctional patterns.

Four Common Breathing Patterns that Contribute to Panic

Are You a Chest Breather?

What happens to the breath during a panic attack? Remember that wild animal running towards you? Your body needs oxygen as fast as possible to allow you to fight hard or run away quickly. How do you get air the fastest way possible? You take a chest breath.

Stand in front of a mirror and observe as you inhale. Are your shoulders and upper chest rising? Can you feel your shoulders and upper chest being lifted upwards when you draw in air? When exaggerated, notice if it looks as if you're gasping for air.

Lifting your chest to take a deep breath may seem normal, but it isn't the natural way to take in air. You may even recall puffing up your chest during a physical exam when the doctor asked you to inhale deeply. But chest breathing equals shallow, inefficient breathing, as you must inhale more quickly to get enough air and only the upper part of the lungs is used. The physiological consequences range from upper body tension to feeling breathless and having a faster heart rate. Close to 100 percent of people who suffer from panic breathe with their chest.

Did you ever watch an infant or small child breathe? Their tiny bellies move up and down. They only take chest breaths while crying or very upset. Older children may still breathe abdominally, but as life becomes more stressful, often during middle school or high school, a shift may occur. Many adults no longer breathe with their bellies. The relaxed breathing pattern of early childhood may give way to a dysfunctional pattern characterized by chest breaths, particularly in those who are prone to anxiety.

With practice, you will use your belly to initiate each breath, just as you did as an infant. Later in this chapter, I'll teach you relaxed, abdominal breathing.

Are You Focusing Too Much on Inhaling?

When feeling short of breath, light-headed, or as if you're about to pass out, you're obviously going to be focused on the need to draw in air. Typically, you're trying to inhale by lifting your chest. But your chest may feel tight and constricted. Then, because you're focused on the need for more air and often worried that your chest is tight and you can't breathe, you lift your chest again to take in another breath. This pattern may be repeated several times. What's wrong with this picture?

You've just hyperventilated! Hyperventilation, or over-breathing, occurs when you inhale, usually rapidly and shallowly, and don't take the time to exhale fully. When breathing normally, you take in oxygen and release carbon dioxide to maintain a proper balance between the two in the bloodstream. Hyperventilation disrupts this balance, resulting in insufficient carbon dioxide compared to oxygen. As a result, arterial blood vessels constrict, causing impaired blood flow.

This dysfunctional pattern may be associated with frequent sighing, a sense of breathlessness, dizziness, light-headedness, numbness or tingling in the extremities, chest pain, or a feeling of unreality. Although typically considered an acute state, it also can be subtle, chronic, and easily overlooked.

When I work with clients in my office, I use biofeedback to show them their breathing in real time on a computer screen. A hyperventilation pattern (exaggerated for demonstration purposes) would look like this:

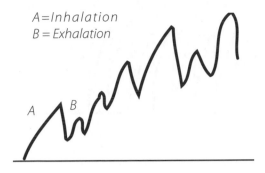

A=Inhalation
B = Exhalation

Notice that rather than making a completed triangle by coming down to the baseline, the right side (B), representing the exhalation, fell short during each breath cycle.

Observe your next breath. As you inhale, notice again if your chest lifts. This time, however, also become aware of the length of the inhalation. Now exhale. Was the inhalation slower or faster than the exhalation? Were they about the same speed?

When hyperventilation occurs during a panic attack, breathing into a paper bag can help. The air you exhale is carbon dioxide, which you then breathe back in. However, using this technique for too long can be counterproductive because you end up with too much carbon dioxide. Rather than becoming dependent on a paper bag, learn to breathe in a relaxed way.

Finding a steady rhythm of breathing by keeping the exhalations as long as the inhalations can prevent hyperventilation. Because exhalation is the most relaxing part of the breath, it's often prolonged so as to fully experience the process of "letting go."

With practice, you'll emphasize and savor the exhalation part of the breath cycle. Later in this chapter, I'll teach you to breathe in and breathe out in an even pattern.

Are You Breathing Too Quickly?

Fast breathing = anxious breathing. During the fight-or-flight response, the body receives a signal that your life is endangered. Why waste time on a slow abdominal breath? Instinctively, you take rapid, shallow breaths while fighting or running away from the danger.

Using biofeedback, a rapid breather would be watching the following pattern being created on the computer screen:

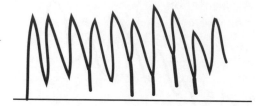

To determine how fast you breathe, time it. Find a watch with a second hand and count each inhalation for one minute.

How many breaths do you take in one minute?

When breathing rapidly, your body works too hard. Slowing down the breath creates a relaxed state. When helping panic sufferers, I used to focus primarily on techniques for learning to breathe abdominally. Now, particularly if clients are struggling with belly breathing, I emphasize breathing rate, which may be the most important ingredient for creating a quieting response. Later in this chapter, I'll teach you ways to slow down the breath.

4 breaths per minute	A blissful, meditative state
5–8 breaths per minute	Relaxed and quiet
9–14 breaths per minute	Engaged in routine tasks or conversation
Over 15 breaths per minute	Running to catch a bus or having a panic attack

Are You Holding Your Breath?

A fourth dysfunctional breathing pattern contributing to panic involves holding your breath completely. Think of a deer caught in headlights. Directly connected to fear, forgetting to breathe is associated with bracing for danger and complete absorption in external events or worrisome thoughts. The consequence of this pattern is insufficient intake of oxygen, including oxygen to the brain, which may be experienced as a closed-in feeling or a sense of being trapped.

For patients who hold their breath, the biofeedback monitoring device picks up the following pattern and displays it on the computer screen like this:

It's often hard to recognize if you're holding your breath. When engaged in an activity that requires physical or mental effort, the likelihood of forgetting to breathe increases. Think of someone trying to lift a heavy object and grunting in the process. Similarly, imagine gasping in surprise upon hearing some unexpected bad news or witnessing something unpleasant.

If you have a timer, set it to go off in five minutes. At the moment that you hear the timer, see if you're in the process of breathing. Repeat this two or three more times in the next half hour. Are you in a holding pattern? Alternately, have someone observe you while you're reading or watching TV. Did they see your stomach or chest moving, or were you in a freeze-frame position?

If you suffer from panic, you're probably holding your breath, thereby blocking the flow of *qi*. As you practice the breathing techniques presented later in this chapter, you'll become aware of a steady, continuous cycle of breath.

Discovering a Healthy Flow of Breath

The process of learning to breathe can be a transformative journey. Imagine that you'll soon be breathing the way you did as a contented infant or a carefree young child. Imagine finding a key that will lead to the elimination of panic.

Let Your Belly Breathe

Abdominal breathing is also known as diaphragmatic breathing. When you push out your belly, the diaphragm, which is a sheet of muscle below your rib cage that is part of your abdominal core, pulls down. This process allows air to be "sucked in" to your lower lungs. When you lift your chest to get air, the diaphragm is not engaged and the air only fills your upper lungs. Abdominal breathing results in getting air into both upper and lower lungs. When exhaling, the diaphragm relaxes and the air is forced out.

Start by placing one hand on your stomach and the other hand on your chest. Take a big breath in and notice if you lifted the hand resting on your chest more than the hand resting on your stomach. Simply observe and feel what moves when you draw in air. Did both hands rise as you took in a breath? Did you lift your shoulders as well as your chest?

Now take the next breath by pushing out your belly so that you can see the hand on your stomach rise. Then, notice it drop down as you draw your belly in towards your spine. You don't need to exaggerate this movement. Find a comfortable expansion and contraction.

Can you see the difference? At this point, just observe your stomach moving out and in. Forget about breathing. If you're thinking to yourself: "I can't breathe with my stomach," "I need to lift my chest to get air," these words will be triggering the alarm system. Instead, tell yourself that learning to breathe abdominally takes practice; you're a beginning student who will master this technique with lots of repetition and a nonjudgmental attitude.

Let go of any thoughts about whether you should be breathing through your nose or mouth. For now, simply push out your belly to take breath in and pull it back to exhale. Think of your stomach as the gills of a fish, breathing automatically. Imagine a baby breathing or picture someone who is sleeping peacefully while taking belly breaths.

Let go of thinking about your breath. Just watch your belly move. Close your eyes and feel it pushing out and drawing back in. Picture the movement. You can also find a mirror and sitting or standing in front of it, watch your stomach breathe for you. While looking at your reflection, glance up at your shoulders. If you observe them moving upwards with each inhalation, then you're probably still breathing with your chest. Tell your shoulders that they're "not needed" right now, and as you push out your belly to take the next breath, feel stillness in your shoulders.

If you're struggling to breathe through your stomach, try practicing while lying down. Again, place one hand on your belly and the other on your upper chest. Expand and contract your stomach and watch your hand rise and fall. When lying down, exhalation becomes easier due to gravity. Think of exhalation in this position as effortless. When sitting or standing it's easier to inhale by sticking your stomach out. Think of inhalation in these positions as effortless.

If you start to feel dizzy, you may be working too hard and consequently breathing too heavily or hyperventilating. Try sticking your belly out a little less as you inhale and relaxing your abdominal muscles more as you exhale to release the air with a little less effort. In fact, let go of effort altogether. Just notice what's happening as you breathe at this moment, good or bad. Tell yourself that soon you'll be taking belly breaths with ease and any dizziness or light-headedness will be history.

If you're still working hard to breathe abdominally, you're over practicing and still engaging effort. You're might be telling yourself, "This isn't working." If so, it's time to take a break. Close this book and find something enjoyable to do. Trust that when you return, you'll find some belly breaths.

When I teach abdominal breathing to people who have been chest breathers all their lives, I usually hear comments such as, "I can't breathe this way. It feels unnatural." I know this feeling well. When I attended my first workshop on relaxation techniques, the class got down on the floor, closed their eyes, and were led through a relaxation exercise that emphasized belly breathing. Because I was a chest breather, I began feeling light-headed and dizzy when I used my stomach to breathe. For years, I inhaled by lifting my chest and contracting my stomach muscles. Now I was being told to do the opposite: inhale by pushing my stomach out and moving the breath from the core. Initially, my chest felt constricted and focusing on abdominal breathing felt unnatural. But I didn't give up; I kept practicing.

Every time I felt nervous, I took some belly breaths and told myself they would take away the jittery feelings. Every time I noticed that I was relaxed, I took some belly breaths to enhance the calmness. After a few weeks of consciously reminding myself to breathe abdominally, I noticed that engaging my core to breathe was becoming easier. That was 36 years ago. Now, abdominal breathing is automatic. When I demonstrate chest breathing, I notice an immediate tightening in my upper chest, neck, shoulders, and even up into the back of my head.

Those new to abdominal breathing often complain, "I'm not getting enough air this way." In reality, belly breathing gives you more air than chest breathing. Long-distance cyclists have been taught to increase their endurance by taking abdominal breaths. Singers and musicians who play wind instruments are taught diaphragmatic breathing to fully utilize their lung capacity. If you try to blow up a balloon only using chest inhalations, you'll transfer significantly less air into the balloon than if you engaged your stomach.

When you resume practicing, try adding imagery to find an abdominal breath. The right image can be a powerful teaching tool, so see if you can connect with the following suggestions:

- Imagine your stomach is a balloon that you're going to inflate with air as you inhale. Then imagine your stomach is a deflating balloon as you exhale. See if you can lose yourself in this image for several more breath cycles. As you continue to imagine your stomach as a balloon inflating and deflating, notice your shoulders. Are they rising and falling with each inhalation and exhalation? If so, tell them to remain still. Notice your thoughts. Is your mind judging, evaluating, or complaining right now? If so, remember that all thoughts and mental images are sorted into darks and lights, safety or danger.

- Replace negative thoughts about how you're breathing with positive, encouraging ones. One way to accomplish this is to tell your mind that it's the observer. Imagine you're doing an experiment and your mind is the scientist. You're simply observing the process of breathing for a nonjudgmental research project. If your mind wanders, bring it back to noticing the very next breath. If you observe that you're breathing with your chest, simply take note of that pattern and take advantage of the following breath to experience an abdominal inhalation.

- Another visualization that I find helpful involves imagining that there's a string attached to your navel and it's being gently pulled outward. Picture that movement as the inhalation. To exhale, imagine there's a string attached to your navel from the inside and you're gently pulling the string towards your spine. To enhance this image, some of you may be old enough to remember the "Chatty Kathy" doll who talked when you pulled the string on her back.

- Dr. James Gordon of the Center for Mind–Body Medicine introduced a very effective strategy called, "soft belly breathing." Simply say to yourself "soft" as you breathe in, and "belly" as you breathe out. As you continue, notice how the softening effect spreads. (One note of caution: make sure that soft isn't negatively interpreted as flabby.)

Now that you're aware of the distinction between a chest breath and a belly breath, let's focus on ways to establish a relaxed breathing pattern.

Find a Steady Rhythm and Savor the Exhalation

Notice the length of each inhalation and exhalation. Remember that hyperventilation occurs when you inhale too much and forget to exhale. From now on I want you to pay attention to breathing out. Notice if you're fully letting go of the air that you took in.

The exhalation is the relaxing part of the breath. It's associated with "letting go." Try starting each breath cycle with an exhalation. Rather than breathing in and breathing out, switch to "breathe out, breathe in." Close your eyes and repeat to yourself several times: "Breathe out, breathe in." Eventually you'll be able to lengthen each exhalation compared to the inhalation. But first we'll focus on evening them out.

The body gets into balance when the breath becomes rhythmical. A relaxing breath is free of pauses or shakiness. Imagining something gliding or flowing smoothly may be helpful. When I want to find balance in a yoga pose, I begin by taking smooth, even breaths.

When clients use biofeedback in my office, they see their breathing pattern on a computer screen. When they fall into a relaxed rhythm, the breath cycle resembles steady, even ocean waves.

Compare this picture to the uneven or jagged spikes created by anxious breathing patterns. During biofeedback sessions, I tell patients to create rolling hills rather than spikes or mountain peaks.

Our imaginations are powerful. You can pretend you're drawing these waves. In your mind's eye, see the gentle rise and fall of waves of water or lush, green rolling hills.

Counting while inhaling and exhaling is another effective tool. Begin by inhaling to a count of 4 and exhaling to a count of 4. If you're comfortable with this pattern, try inhaling to a count of 5 and exhaling to a count of 5.

As you exhale, try letting out the breath through your teeth, creating a soft, hissing sound. You can also exhale as if you were blowing out a candle. Now try a few breath cycles where you purse your lips and pretend you're lightly blowing on a feather or sunflower while letting the air out. Because sighing is associated with pleasure or release, experiment by adding a big sigh as you exhale. Have you noticed that these actions may be causing the exhalations to grow longer than the inhalations?

If you want to return to counting, inhale to the count of 4 and extend the exhalation to 5. Then inhale to a count of 4 and exhale to a count of 7 or 8. There's no correct number or pattern. Pick what feels comfortable right now and then play with elongating the count on the exhalations. For fun, count in a different language, vary between odd and even numbers, or choose a number with a special meaning.

At this point I haven't told you how fast to count. But you can probably guess where we're going.

S...L...O...W   D...O...W...N   Y...O...U...R
B...R...E...A...T...H...I...N...G

Based on both personal and professional experience, I believe that slowing down your breathing is the best way to stop a panic attack. Taking your foot off the accelerator and applying the brakes to runaway breathing eases you into belly breathing and signals the parasympathetic nervous system to take over.

Picture a closed accordion. That's how the breath pattern looks when you're anxious. Imagine opening up the accordion. Picture even waves spaced far apart.

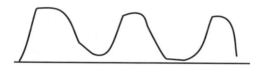

Why is slower better?

- Taking slow, deep breaths stops hyperventilation.

- Taking slow, deep breaths focuses attention on the breath and not the panic.

- Taking slow, deep breaths quiets the heart.

- Taking slow, deep breaths calms the mind.

When you slow down to approximately six breaths per minute, or ten seconds per breath, you'll be breathing at an ideal rate. This rate of breathing results in optimum heart-rate variability, the beat-to-beat changes in the heart's rhythms, which we'll discuss in greater detail in a later chapter.

To experience a ten-second breath cycle, begin by looking at a watch or clock with a second hand timer. Breathe in for five seconds and breathe out for five seconds. Are you inflating your belly to inhale? Are you contracting it to exhale? Try pursing your lips and exhaling gently for the five seconds. The next step is to inhale for four seconds and exhale for six seconds. Continue for the next several breath cycles. Now close your eyes and stay with this rhythm and speed of breath. If you're not sure of the timing, count "1 one thousand, 2 one thousand, 3 one thousand, 4 one thousand" as you inhale and "6 one thousand, 5 one thousand, 4 one thousand, 3 one thousand, 2 one thousand, 1 one thousand" as you exhale.

To become even more relaxed, pause for about a half a second to a second for a hold after inhaling, then exhale and pause again for a similar hold before drawing in another breath.

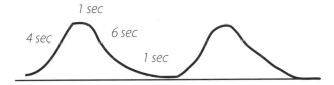

Are you still unsure of how to breathe in a slow, relaxed way, or do you have clients who may need a more structured approach? Fortunately, help is available. I tell clients that biofeedback offers a "high-tech" way to learn to relax. Portable biofeedback devices that are relatively inexpensive can be purchased for use at home or at work.

There are two biofeedback trainers that I recommend for reinforcing a relaxed breathing pattern. The first is the Emwave Personal Stress Reliever, a small, hand-held gadget that reads your heart rhythms through a finger or ear sensor to detect pulse and give immediate feedback. A breathing coach guides you to a relaxed respiratory pattern. A second home trainer is the Resperate, a device originally studied for control of hypertension. Similar to the Emwave, the unit provides feedback so you can achieve a breath cycle of about six breaths per minute (see Appendix 1: Resources).

A third option involves downloading a software program called EZ-Air Plus on your computer (see Appendix 1: Resources). A ball moving up and down a line graph helps you pace your inhalations and exhalations. If you own a smartphone, there are several breathing pacers now available as downloadable applications and more sophisticated versions are continually being developed.

Breathe Continuously

Clients frequently want to know how often they should practice slow, relaxed breathing. Tell them that their breath accompanies them wherever they go. Either an inhalation or an exhalation can initiate every movement. That's how yoga is practiced.

As a beginner, start with defined times, such as upon awakening, at bedtime, while taking a break at work, when ending a phone call, while waiting in line, or before and after every meal (which will dramatically improve digestion). I tell clients to tune in to their breathing whenever they have some free moments.

- Practice when you're comfortable, happy or content.

- When you walk outside and it's a beautiful day, enhance the positive experience by taking an abdominal breath.

- To savor a special moment, take a deep belly breath.

- When you pair positive thoughts with abdominal breathing, you're establishing a strong mind–body connection.

- Practicing during good times prepares you for finding relaxed breathing when panicky feelings emerge.

- Consciously pausing to find a deep belly breath breaks the habit of holding your breath. Once you discover relaxed breathing, it's easier to catch periods of holding in.

- Focusing on the breath during a panic episode distracts you from the scary feelings.

- Focusing on the breath grounds you in the present moment, as your breath cycle is happening right now. Remember that anxiety is connected to a future event.

- Can you find 20 seconds for two breath cycles? How soon after noticing an anxious feeling can you take a slow, belly breath? Stay with the breath and soon you'll feel like a huge weight has been lifted off your chest.

Count Your Breaths
COUNTING BACKWARDS

A tried-and-true technique, counting backwards consists of pairing a number with an exhalation. Try counting from 20 down to 1. If that's not working, try going from 10 to 1. To really distract yourself, count backwards from 100 by 9s.

THE 4-7-8 BREATH CYCLE

At the Integrative Mental Health Conference in March of 2010, I attended a breathing workshop with Dr. Andrew Weil. He led participants through a structured breathing exercise that he described as his personal favorite for attaining a profound quieting response.

- Begin with an exhalation.

- Then breathe in through your nose as you count slowly to 4.

- Hold your breath as you count to 7.

- Exhale through your mouth as you count to 8.

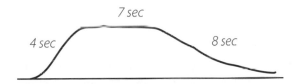

Repeat this pattern four times. After the fourth cycle, go back to the normal rhythm of slow, relaxed belly breathing.

Practice these four cycles of breath twice a day for four weeks, then either move on to eight cycles of breath or stay with four. Practice first thing in the morning and before bed. Feel your hands warm, your heart rate slow, and anxiety melt away. What makes this pattern particularly beneficial? The vagus nerve is stimulated during the 7 count hold and signals the autonomic nervous system to shift into a relaxation response.

Breathe with Imagination

Focusing on the breath can be a wonderful distraction from disturbing, anxiety-producing thoughts. Initiate slow belly breathing, and the alarm system shuts off. In the absence of a danger signal, the quieting response takes over.

What if you're trying to slow down your breathing and take belly breaths, but you still feel anxious and panicky and doubt that breathing techniques will work for you? What if focusing on breathing makes you more anxious and panicky? Both of these outcomes are common, particularly for those who are new to mind–body relaxation.

- The process of change begins with imagination. Pretend that slow, abdominal breathing will help you become calmer.

- Imagine the breath sending out signals to your nervous system, telling it to calm down.

- Imagine that the breath is whisper soft and soothing. Go with the image of "soothing" and associate it with something else that feels soothing.

- Imagine the breath moving all the way down to your fingers and toes. Pretend that your fingers and toes are becoming warm and relaxed.

- Imagine something agitated, such as a stormy sea. Now picture a very calm, smooth body of water as you create waves of slow, abdominal breaths.

- Imagine the warmth of the breath flowing through your heart. Pretend your chest is "melting" or softening every time you exhale.

- Imagine inhaling feelings of wellbeing.

- Imagine the scary, panicky sensations being exhaled along with the breath.

- Imagine breathing as a child.

- Imagine inhaling equanimity.

- Imagine letting go of any jerkiness in the breath cycle.

- Imagine something that flows, such as flower petals, tall grasses swaying in a gentle breeze, or dancers swaying back and forth.

If you like using words, say to yourself: "I am" as you inhale and "calm" or "relaxed" as you exhale. But why not be creative? Say, "I love" as you inhale, and the name of a favorite person, place, or activity as you exhale.

Imagine Breathing Past Your Spine

Another powerful breathing technique involves exhaling into your back body. This is one of my personal favorites for letting go of tension, because it's possible to imagine quieting your adrenal glands. These two "baby" glands sit above the kidneys and secrete the stress hormones associated with activation of the sympathetic response. The surge of adrenaline fuels a panic attack, while cortisol is largely responsible for the feeling of being "keyed up" and on edge.

Place your hands on your lower back while seated or lying down. As you exhale, feel your navel moving back towards your spine. Now imagine your breath continuing beyond your spine and puffing out your lower back. With your hands on your back, you may actually feel your back expand into your hands.

Imagine your breath is creating a cushion for your adrenal glands. You can also imagine the air inflating your lower back, as if creating an inner tube. As you breathe into your lower back, your abdominal muscles are actually creating a "lock" so that your lower back is protected during movement.

Exhale and feel your lower back puffing up. Visualize the breath soothing your overworked adrenal glands. Imagine you're replenishing your supply of cortisol. When you're in a relaxed state, this is what actually happens!

Teach Children to Breathe While Playing

Have Soap Bubbles Handy

Explanations about breathing can be boring and children may have a hard time focusing their attention on a wordy therapist. Children learn effectively via play. A great way to teach abdominal breathing is to make it fun and playful. One of my favorite methods involves the use of soap bubbles.

Begin by showing the child (or adult) how to blow strongly in order to produce big bubbles. First take a chest breath, then a stomach breath. Which produced the better bubble? Suggest creating a huge bubble by blowing the soap through the ring while simultaneously keeping one hand on the belly to feel it moving. When dipping the wand into the bottle, emphasize slowly inhaling. Count from 1 to 4 while exhaling a giant bubble. Either gradually extend the count to 8 or slow down the 4-count rhythm. By proceeding slowly, one large bubble can be produced that won't pop. Notice the bubbles drifting farther away. Playing with this image, place specific fears into the bubbles and watch them disintegrate.

Give Toys a Belly Ride

When working with young children, I have them place a small stuffed animal over their bellies and give their friend a ride. As one little girl told me, "It's important to go slowly because I wouldn't want to give my bear motion sickness from going too fast." What better way to remember to keep the breathing process slow and steady!

Be Silly and Playful

Maybe you feel silly giving a stuffed animal a ride on your belly. How about using a book or another object instead? (To enhance the experience, choose a favorite one.) As you inhale, let your stomach push against the weight of the book. See the book lift when inflating your belly to inhale and watch it being lowered as you exhale. Remember to breathe slowly. Imagine the book balanced precariously and you don't want to let it fall over. Choose to close your eyes and feel the movement, if you so desire.

Can you recreate the relaxing scene pictured below?

Enhance the relaxation effect by imagining settling into a hammock with an opened book at your private getaway in beautiful Hawaii!

In the next chapter, we'll take a closer look at the power of imagery, but first here's a summary of the key points presented so far.

Summing It All Up

Breathing is the key to overcoming panic and creating a relaxation response, but stress and anxiety constrict the flow of breath.

Teach clients to say to themselves: "I'm not physically or mentally ill, it's my breathing that's off. I can control my breathing and wait for the panic to subside."

Four altered breathing patterns contribute to panic:

- shallow chest breathing

- inhaling more than exhaling

- breathing too rapidly

- holding the breath.

What's the best way to stop a panic attack?

- find belly breaths

- focus on exhaling

- breathe in slow motion, around six breaths per minute.

What if after shoveling a driveway full of snow so many years ago, I paused to enjoy slow abdominal breaths, savoring the exhalations rather than focusing on fear? I could have relaxed and enjoyed the beauty of the fresh snow instead of bringing on a severe panic attack and landing in the emergency room.

CHAPTER 4

Imagine Something Good

Finding Positive Connections

"Imagination is more important than knowledge."
—*Albert Einstein*

What if practicing relaxed breathing during an anxiety attack isn't helpful? Most likely the trouble stems from expecting that taking a breath will automatically lead to a particular outcome, in this case, stopping a panic attack. The mind saying, "I'm going to try this breathing technique that my doctor taught me and see if it works to calm me down" resembles thinking, "I'm going to take this pill and see if it relaxes me." The mind is busy working to achieve a goal.

In order for slow, abdominal breathing to initiate a relaxation response, both mind and body need to be fully engaged in the process of shutting off the alarm system. This process involves imagining "garden hoses" rather than "snakes."

Imagining feeling good harnesses so much power that it can even influence the effectiveness of medications. It's called the placebo effect, which has been credited with creating positive changes that are more powerful than prescription drugs.

A vivid imagination shuts the danger signal off and switches the safety signal on, but many people don't use it to their advantage because they're hyperfocusing on how miserable they feel. When stuck in irrational, obsessive thoughts, I often ask them to shift to observing a warm feeling. If that suggestion only produces more negativity, recalling childhood fun can sometimes be a good place to start. Try using the following script:

Remember how you used your imagination when you were a child? Did you pretend you were a princess or a superhero? Did you put on a costume or play dress up and imagine you were that person?" Did you build entire cities from blocks? Did you draw and turn simple shapes into elaborate scenes? Did you make up stories?

During a panic attack you're using the same imaginative powers that you used when you engaged in pretend play. You're imagining something negative and the body responds, so you feel worse. Now we're going to let go of those dark images to bring on positive ones. To enrich the experience, we'll incorporate all of the senses: sight, sound, touch, smell, and taste. We'll also access powerful heartfelt emotions such as appreciation, compassion, and gratitude.

What if your clients can't imagine childhood, and you don't want to go there because they may associate that time with traumatic experiences, or they tell you they're "bad at imagining"? Point out that although they will learn to use their imagination to create what they want, at present they're masters at imagining in a negative way.

As a panic sufferer you have a strong imagination and get an A+ in imagining the negative. I bet you can imagine the worst perfectly. You're probably great at picturing your limitations, obstacles, past problems, and qualities you believe you're lacking.

Encourage clients to view the process of developing imagery as magical, for the potential exists to experience changes that will be transformational. No matter where they're starting from, anyone can learn to harness the power of imagination and observe the calm state that soon develops. By combining belly breathing with creative imagery, you can guide others towards creating profound changes, often in a short amount of time. Change doesn't come about by thinking, planning, and worrying. Change is a mind–body–spirit process.

The process of creating positive imagery has no guidelines or boundaries. So where to begin? Sometimes the best place to start is far away from the intention to control panic. Just give permission to daydream. Here are some possibilities:

- Imagine somewhere you would like to be.
- Imagine an event that you would like to attend.
- Imagine something you want to have happen.

- Imagine someone you want to be with.

- Imagine a song you like.

- Imagine the taste of something you like to eat.

- Imagine something good from your childhood.

- Imagine what you ate this morning.

For young children or someone who is quite literal, try beginning at a basic level by picturing colors and shapes. Take it further by imagining them flowing and morphing from one to another. Whether working with children or adults, getting out a drawing pad and some markers, watercolors, or crayons may enhance this experience. Expressing oneself through art is usually a great way to unleash creative imagination.

Try On Relaxation

While the suggestions described above are open-ended and general, it's also possible to get someone into the habit of imagining his/her life in a relaxed state. The following questions could be posed when you hear the familiar retort, "I'm an anxious person":

- How would you be if you were a relaxed person?

- How would you feel and act?

- How would you relate to your family and friends?

- How would you behave differently at work?

- Where would you travel?

- What new hobbies would you try?

- What new learning would you pursue?

- How would you express your creativity?

- Does being a relaxed person appeal to you?

- What would wellbeing feel like?

I often ask clients to imagine being a relaxed person free of panic attacks:

If you now think of yourself as a panic attack sufferer or as someone with anxiety, imagine erasing or deleting these characterizations. Imagine shedding the burden of anxiety the way you would let go of a heavy package that you've been carrying. If you've been diagnosed with panic disorder or anxiety disorder, imagine obliterating these diagnoses. Imagine that your physician never uttered those words.

Imagine assuming the characteristics of someone who is relaxed and easy going. If you were an actor and had to play the part, how would you stand? How would your limbs feel? How would you hold your jaw? How would you breathe?

Maybe create your own version of the following message:

Remember what it was like to pretend? Pretend that you're very relaxed. When you start to feel panicked or anxious, pretend that you're feeling fine. This process involves more than simply saying "I'm fine" to yourself, although that's a good start. Using your imagination involves taking on the role of a relaxed person in every fiber of your being.

Imagine what you want exactly as you want it. Think of the details and create it just as you would like it to be. What would your shoulders feel like? How would you stand? How would you walk? How would you breathe? How confident would you feel? Can you live your life as if you were better?

Remember a time when you were extremely relaxed and imagine feeling that way now. How old were you? Where were you at the time? Imagine the sights, sounds, smells, and textures that surrounded you. Pretend you're there now.

If you hear the common retort, "I can't think of a time when I was relaxed" or "There was never a time when I didn't feel anxious," direct attention to the awareness that these thoughts are moving their entire being into the danger zone. Encourage changing direction, taking a 360-degree turn by shifting to rational thinking. Guide them to the conclusion: "I'm not anxious 100 percent of the time, every single waking and sleeping moment of my life. How about when I was an infant?"

The body knows how to relax because it's an innate biological response. We relaxed as infants, lost ourselves in imaginative play and relaxed as children, and the body can relax in the middle of a panic attack. When evoking positive imagery, the judging part of the brain turns off and the body begins to quiet.

Ideally, we want to find a state of balance. Although we've talked a lot about relaxation, creating imagery is not just about finding relaxation. We're moving towards experiencing a combination of relaxation and strength, stability, and flexibility. The image of a tree is a good one because we can feel the strength and firmness of the roots and trunk as well as the lightness and flexibility of the branches and leaves. The hardiness of a plant, one that can't be uprooted by a strong wind, is another powerful metaphor.

When I work with young children with fears and anxiety, using the image of becoming their favorite superhero can be very effective. What representations of strength, courage, or fortitude occur to you at this moment?

Consciously Choose What You Wish to Create

I received my doctorate in clinical psychology from Fielding Graduate University. One unique aspect of the program stands out more than all the coursework put together. Newly enrolled students met in a small group and were asked to travel about ten years into the future to a class reunion. I introduced myself as "Dr. Scheinbaum" and described my accomplishments. Others in the group addressed me as "Dr. Scheinbaum." The power of that exercise resided in the rich emotional imagery it evoked. We were imagining ourselves as becoming Ph.D. psychologists. Returning to that exercise at times when it seemed as though graduating was an impossibility helped to sustain the forward momentum.

Émile Coué (1857–1926), a French psychologist and pharmacist, believed that imagination was much more powerful than willpower. He encouraged his patients to repeat to themselves the famous saying, "Every day in every way, I am getting better and better." This aphorism may sound corny today, but not the underlying message: trust in the process of getting better; trust that the mind and body can change, trust that you and your client are creating a powerful alliance to facilitate change. The thinking mind can't make it happen, but positive connections can.

When the mind creates a movie of favorite places, positive emotions are experienced. Try it yourself. Begin by allowing your imagination to find a place you would like to visit, either real or a fantasy. Let your fantasy happen: build it and create your mental movie step by step. As you read through the suggestions that follow, notice your personal reactions. Feel free to add more images. Then imagine encouraging your clients to trust their creative imaginations to transport them to positive places.

The Power of Nature

Reconnecting with nature is one of the most popular ways to create a relaxation response. As the senses are awakened, joyful feelings typically emerge. When the heart and mind are busy experiencing a sense of wonder, there's no space for anxiety.

While writing this chapter, I'm visiting my cousin in Big Sky, Montana. I'm sitting outside in a rocking chair on a beautiful deck overlooking dense forests and the Rocky Mountains in the distance. My own state of inner quiet can mirror the beauty and complete peacefulness of the surroundings. I can take a mental snapshot and retrieve this memory anywhere and at any time. Remember, what's real in the mind is real in the body. If I recreate this scene, my body will become as relaxed as it feels at this moment.

Take some time to paint a mental picture of your own favorite settings before encouraging clients to engage in this process. What natural surroundings do you associate with joy and serenity? Photographs and paintings of beautiful landscapes can serve as taking-off points for imagining being in these locations at this very moment in time. Find a scene that you like and step into it with full sensory awareness. Place yourself somewhere in the picture and let the spirit move you.

Try exploring the following images or scenes:

- a brilliant sunrise or sunset
- a favorite beach
- a forest of towering pine trees
- a blossoming tree
- a beautiful butterfly
- snow gently falling
- the sound of rain on a roof while you're safe and warm inside.

Now enrich these images. How about a sunrise or sunset over a lake? Can you see the stillness of the water? What sounds can you hear in the distance? Can you feel a gentle breeze across your face? Imagine lying on a beautiful beach. Can you feel the sand beneath you and hear the sounds of the ocean? Can you picture the waves and imagine your breath is creating that same wave pattern?

Again, what's real in the mind is real in the body. Where do you want to go in your mind? Take a fantasy trip. What do you want to imagine or pretend? The mind can begin with one comforting image and travel on as one association leads to another.

How about following the butterfly through a garden? Is it sunny outside? Can you zoom in and see colors? Picture the garden awakening. Zoom in on one flower in your mind and watch it sway in the light breeze. Add a bird's song.

Take an imaginary nature walk and let it be a sensory experience. Look at the sky; notice the sun filtering through the trees. Observe the various colors of the leaves and the shape of tree limbs. Feel the firmness of the earth beneath your feet, the breeze touching your skin. Imagine feeling pure joy as you notice signs of life all around. Experience the stillness of the surroundings. Pretend you're drifting on a canoe in calm waters. Imagine recreating that stillness within you at this moment.

Take in the sights, sounds and smells of a meadow. Now stand on a hill overlooking the meadow. How about traveling all the way to the top of a tall mountain? Lift your arms up to the sky and feel complete joy. Imagine being filled up with that power.

If you're in the mood for a different season, imagine walking in newly fallen snow. Observe the white world that surrounds you. See the tracks you're creating. Feel the stillness, the quiet that surrounds you and imagine recreating that inside you right now. Make snow angels. Build a snowman or a fort. See yourself laughing and being silly. See yourself as strong and invincible.

Going Indoors to Cozy Places

Not everyone enjoys being outdoors. Some people have physical pain or limitations and can't travel to the places described above. Panic sufferers may prefer the safety of an indoor setting. Imagine the following scenes and make them come alive, as if you were creating a 3D movie:

- Imagine sitting inside and taking in a wonderful vista.

- Imagine watching snow falling.

- Imagine observing the movement of the clouds.

- Imagine looking out and seeing the most brilliant display of fall colors.

- Imagine trees or flowers outside your window.

- Imagine sitting beside a window and basking in a pool of sunlight on a cold, wintry day.

- Take the preceding image further and imagine sitting by a sunny window as if you were a lazy cat curled up on a rug or windowsill.

If the marvels of nature just don't cut it or you can't stop thinking about the lack of a beautiful view from your own windows, move to an interior view instead.

- Can you picture your childhood room?

- Can you recreate the kitchen of your childhood home?

- Can you imagine a roaring fireplace?

- How about visualizing a beautiful bathroom with an inviting bathtub?

- Envision a cozy nook for reading.

- Imagine watching a burning candle or an array of candles of all shapes and sizes.

Once the location is established, let your imagination go and fill in the details. If you like remembering your childhood room, can you fill the room with your favorite stuffed animals, dolls, toys? What did cuddling in your bed under your blanket feel like? Do you want to turn on your favorite music from that time period? Can you imagine the texture of your pillow, the scent? Can you see the color and feel the texture of the comforter or blanket on your bed?

Can you imagine the smell of soup cooking on the stove providing satisfying nourishment on a cold, rainy day? Can you imagine the aroma of bread baking in the oven? Are there other aromatic pleasures that you want to surround yourself with? Do you want to imagine being served a wonderful meal at a beautifully set table that has been prepared just for you?

Can you imagine sitting by the fireplace? Do you feel warmth emanating from the fire? Can you hear the crackling of the logs? Can you watch the dancing of the flames?

Can you feel the water as you lean back and soak in the tub? Do you want to add an essential oil? How about candles? Do you want scented candles? Would music add something special to the scene? Feel the warmth and pretend it's enveloping you right now. Imagine your skin softening. Pretend you're warming and softening on the inside as well.

Imagine growing something or planting an indoor herb garden. What herbs come to mind? Take a big, belly breath and draw in their scents. How about gathering some chamomile, mint, lemon balm or lavender fresh from your garden, putting it into a tea ball and steeping it? Inhale the steam from the tea. Feel soothed. Maybe you prefer smelling fresh basil or rosemary? Where does your imagination go now? My mind drifts to making pesto and roasting vegetables with rosemary and garlic.

Recreate Pleasurable Physical Sensations

What's real in the mind becomes real in the body. We've all experienced pleasure on a physical level. Notice if it's easy or difficult for you to access these feelings. Are there any emotional blocks to letting in pleasure? It's impossible to feel pleasure and pain at exactly the same moment. If you immersed yourself in the fantasy of soaking in the tub, you were recreating a pleasurable sensation. Once you're comfortable with feeling physical pleasure, you can guide others towards accessing this sensation.

I'm writing while sitting outside. It's a hot summer afternoon and I hear the sounds of my neighbors splashing in their pool next door. Hearing these sounds, my mind wanders to how great I feel while swimming: I love seeing the sparkling water, imagining how refreshingly cool it feels, noticing each movement as I glide through the water. Creating the mental fantasy only takes about a minute, but that minute nourishes the brain as sympathetic arousal is reduced and parasympathetic activity increases.

Can you take any of the following suggestions and create your own multi-sensory fantasy?

- Imagine getting a wonderful massage.

- Imagine swimming.

- Imagine floating on a raft in a beautiful pool.

- Imagine riding a bicycle.

- Imagine dancing.

- Imagine having great sex.

Add Special People and Pets

Nature's wonders can fill us with awe and help create stillness in mind and body, but imagining people and pets takes the relaxation response to a deeper level because the heart is engaged.

- Take any of the fantasy trips you created above and add someone special to the scene. Add a group of people.

- Simply imagine the faces of people you love, as if you were viewing a slide show.

- Imagine holding a baby against your chest. Feel her warmth and softness. Notice her sweet smells. Imagine her warmth penetrating and warming your chest.

- Imagine your pet resting on your lap. Notice the warmth of her body. Stroke her fur. Feel her breathing.

I remember being called in to see a hospitalized patient who was diagnosed with metastatic cancer and experiencing anxiety and pain. I led her through an abdominal breathing process and she immediately associated images of warmth with having her beloved cat resting peacefully on her belly. As she closed her eyes, she felt the warmth from her cat soothing her both physically and emotionally. This image also helped her maintain abdominal breathing.

Find Stillness by Listening to Surrounding Noises

I've presented lots of possibilities for exploring creative imagery. You allowed your mind to wander and experienced some peaceful sensations. But you might be saying to yourself, "enough already," or you may have concluded that the population you work with is just too anxious to let their minds wander towards fantasy. If that's the case, let's turn to some alternatives. Leave the foreground, pull the focus away from the center of the stage, and tune in to the background: the sounds emanating from the sidelines.

Most clinicians who teach relaxation want to provide quiet surroundings. Books on relaxation usually suggest beginning the process by finding a quiet place. I'm not a big fan of searching for a quiet environment. Because I often rent office space from physicians, I've led clients through relaxation protocols in medical exam rooms while seated in uncomfortable chairs and hearing loud conversations just outside the door. I want clients to find inner quiet wherever they are. Find it in the middle of the New York Stock Exchange, at a busy airport, in Times Square or Trafalgar Square, while standing in line at the grocery store, or at a soccer game, a football stadium, a crowded store, or a rock concert. These are the places where panic might develop. Just as panic can occur anywhere, anytime, anyplace, you can relax anywhere, anytime, anyplace. So embrace the sounds of your current surroundings to find inner quiet.

Another reason why I don't only suggest practicing relaxation in quiet areas, aside from the fact that they may not be available when needed, is that the artificially imposed stillness may result in the volume of the critical, judging mind being turned up. Before you know it, anxiety-producing thoughts awaken. Sometimes we purposely want attention drawn towards the background noise, not inwardly towards our thoughts.

Listening to room tones is a wonderful way to remain in the present moment. These sounds are happening now. Just close your eyes and tune in, as if you're a radio receiver. What can you pick up? Hear the background noises we typically try to tune out. Right now, I'm sitting in an outdoor plaza and hear an airplane overhead, conversations a few feet away that sound like whispers, and traffic in the distance. Perhaps you hear cars passing by or notice the sounds from an air-conditioning system or heater, or the creaking of the floorboards. A young client who had just tuned in to background noises as a relaxation technique described the experience as "listening to a symphony."

A wonderful game for anchoring someone in the present is "I Spy." For example, "I spy something red." Then the other person has to look around the area and find that something red. This can be engaged in with all the senses. For example, "I spy something blowing," or "I spy something cold." Try engaging a child who is anxious by directing attention to what is happening within the immediate surroundings. The distraction of playing this game quiets the alarm response and prevents mental time travel to the past or future; plus it's a lot of fun.

Many years ago, I worked with an adolescent girl who closed her eyes, found the sounds coming from nearby medical equipment (noise I interpreted as annoying and an obstacle to the relaxation process), and somehow turned it into a creative fantasy about a waterfall. She went on to imagine the waterfall sending cooling water down her arms, a process which helped reduce the painful burning she was experiencing from reflex sympathetic dystrophy. Once again, prejudging or forgetting to trust that change happens when you don't plan for it restrains the natural healing process.

Creating Guided Imagery Scripts

I'm not a big fan of ready-made guided imagery, because the best creative imagining occurs spontaneously. There can also be pitfalls associated with scripts, which are described at the end of this chapter. However, they come in handy when clients ask for something structured to listen to that can guide them into a relaxed state.

The key to a successful guided imagery experience is complete immersion in the fantasy trip that's presented. Follow the opening lines of a possible script:

Choose a place to relax that is uniquely satisfying to you. Imagine a beach, a garden, a cabin in the mountains, or a private hideaway. Pay attention to whatever fantasy occurs to you at this moment. Perhaps you're swimming, fishing, planting flowers, conversing with good friends, or sitting by a fireplace with a good book.

Now you take it from there. Close your eyes and step into this movie. Embellish the scene by adding colors, sounds, smells, tastes and additional footage. Notice the places where your mind wants to go and let the fantasy unfold.

Picture a scene in your mind's eye where you are comfortable, safe, and relaxed, a place where you can leave the outside pressures and demands behind. You might imagine yourself in some location in which you were relaxed in the past, perhaps while on vacation or lying on a chaise longue in your yard. You could also choose to create an image of your ideal vacation or fantasy. Make your mental movie come alive by using all your senses.

A popular guided visualization takes you to the beach. It usually starts out something like this:

Imagine descending a long staircase and finding yourself at a beautiful beach. Observe the color of the water, see the horizon in the distance, hear the sound of the waves and the seagulls flying over the ocean, feel the sand between your toes. Find a comfortable chair, put down your belongings, and settle in as you close your eyes and bask in the warming rays of the sun.

A path in the woods or leading up to a mountain offers many possibilities for creative imagery:

As you walk along, see the tall trees, smell the ground beneath you, the smell of earth. Notice the colors of any wildflowers beside the path. See the blue sky through the treetops. Hear rushing water off in the distance. Come to a mountain stream or a waterfall. Pause to take in your surroundings: the sights, the smells, and the sounds. Continue walking along the path until you arrive at the top of a hill. What do you see as you look out over the hill? This can be your special place to relax and you can return anytime you want to.

I encourage you to create a few guided imagery scripts. Just close your eyes and paint a mental picture. Record it, perhaps on the voice memo application on your phone (a great way to access your voice quality, pacing, and inflection if you plan to make a recording for others to listen to), or write it down. Then listen with your eyes closed in a comfortable position. Encourage clients to do this as well. Make it a collaborative process.

With children, developing a guided imagery script can start as a storytelling game. You initiate by taking them on a journey to a special place. After a defined amount of time (typically about one minute using a watch with a second hand), it's their turn to embellish the scene. When it's your turn, add soothing sights, sounds, smells, and textures. Be sure to include family, friends, and animals. Continue back and forth for enough rounds to create a magical place that they can revisit when upset or scared. I often make recordings of these stories that children can listen to at night before getting into bed.

Playing with the Breath

Let's get back to breathing. Positive imagery and relaxed breathing go hand in hand. Breathing creates the foundation for wellbeing, but blending creative imagery with breathing strengthens and deepens this process. Creating imagery about breathing is a good place to start. Try the following suggestions yourself and then present them to someone else:

- As you push out your belly to take in a breath, turn your attention to the air just outside your nostrils. Notice how it feels. Can you imagine it tickling your nostrils? Is it rushing in like a strong gust of wind? Can you slow it down until it becomes a gentle breeze coming through an open window?

- Notice the temperature of the air you inhale. Does it feel cool?

- Feeling warm or overheated is common during or just before a panic attack, so imagining inhaling cool, refreshing air is a great fantasy to get lost in. When the imagination is unleashed, the mind can go anywhere. Going further, how about suggesting associating cool air with that wonderful feeling of stepping into a cool air-conditioned place when you're very hot. This image, or pretending there's a cool breeze coming in from an open window, works wonders when one is in a hot room, a high-risk place for panic to develop.

- How about the movement of air from an overhead circulating fan? What associations does that image evoke? Does walking by the ocean enjoying the clean, cool fresh air create a pleasant feeling? Give clients permission to let their minds travel to all sorts of wonderful places associated with cool air, always returning to inhaling coolness.

- What about the opposite? What's it like to imagine the warmth of the breath? We usually associate warmth with something soothing.

- As you exhale by pulling your navel towards your spine, imagine that your body has warmed the air you inhaled. Imagine that your belly is a furnace that's warming the air you've taken in. Feel the soothing warmth of the breath flow through you.

- Imagine feeling comfortably warm, experiencing the warmth of snuggling under a cozy blanket when it's cold outside.

- Imagine warm oil on your skin or the feeling of warm hands when getting a massage.

- Imagine being on a beautiful beach and walking on warm sand.

- Imagine your breath as creating a warm inner glow.

- As you draw in air, imagine inhaling something warm and calming.

- As you exhale, imagine this warm, soothing substance spreading from head to toe.

In with the Good, Out with the Bad

If you greet each client without a predetermined agenda, you'll be practicing mindfulness and sensing what's needed in the present moment. Working without a lesson plan also implies that there will be unexpected twists and turns. It means trusting your own creative imagination. I use every encounter with a client as an opportunity to relax on a personal level and let go of feeling tense, upset, worried, rushed, or out of balance. By taking some slow belly breaths, I'm able to center myself in the moment and let go of any expectations or judgments. Through mindful awareness, I'm able to stay attuned to what's positive and trust that any healing images or messages I want to convey will emerge. In a nutshell, we're both practicing letting in something good and letting go of something bad.

Try using this image to practice:

Imagine what you need right now and inhale it with the next breath. Imagine what you want to get rid of and exhale it along with the stale air.

Or experiment with being more specific:

Imagine inhaling feelings of peacefulness. Imagine exhaling little bits of the panicky feeling.

Any sensation that feels good can be breathed into the body, including joy, lightness, steadiness, balance, calmness, strength, flexibility, warmth, coolness, or a complete sense of equanimity.

As you inhale with your belly, draw in full deep breaths of joy. Imagine joy coming into every pore on your skin, as if your skin was one big breathing organ.

As you inhale, breathe in feelings of lightness in your belly and your upper body, as if you're lifting a heavy burden off your chest and creating more breathing space. As your exhale, feel grounded and a sense of steadiness through your lower body, as if you're firmly planted or rooted.

With each breath, imagine the feeling of equanimity growing stronger.

Stay with the feeling. It will dissolve after a few seconds. Go back to your breath and feel it again.

Another strategy consists of adding images to contrast panic and relaxation.

Imagine pushing your panic away. Give it a shape and color.

Now imagine a color and shape for relaxation. Imagine the shape and color of the panic changing to the shape and color of relaxation.

Similarly, imagine bright lights. Assign panic the color red and choose green for relaxation. Imagine the lights changing from red to purple to blue and finally to a beautiful shade of green.

Breathing Through the Heart

"There is no reason not to follow your heart."
—*Steve Jobs*

To experience a complete sense of peacefulness, the heart and brain need to be in harmony with one another. While medical textbooks describe the heart in terms of its physiological function, our emotional sense of the heart is quite different. Rather than simply pumping blood, the heart plays a central role in how we think and feel. Positive feelings in the heart create a ripple that sends wellbeing throughout the body. We want to access its intelligence and power to lead us to a clear, peaceful state of awareness; we want to follow our hearts.

Dating back thousands of years, yogi masters, poets and philosophers have referred to the heart as the center of life, the internal "guru." Science now confirms that the heart has its own nervous system, which relays information back to the brain, creating a two-way communication process. Heartbeats are actually an intelligent language, as these rhythmic beating patterns are transformed into neural impulses that directly affect the higher brain centers. More specifically, as the heartbeat changes, so does electrical activity in the amygdala, the part of the brain responsible for processing emotions.

Heart-rate variability patterns, the measurements of the beat-to-beat changes in heart rate, also referred to as heart rhythms, are powerful direct reflections of our inner emotional state. Increasing heart-rate variability reduces the activity of the sympathetic nervous system and increases the activity of the parasympathetic branch. By accessing feelings such as compassion, appreciation, and forgiveness, heart-rate variability increases, rhythmical breathing ensues, and the parasympathetic branch keeps the stress response in check. This process can be thought of as keeping the brake on (the parasympathetic response) to prevent the alarm from going off (the sympathetic response). By accessing a positive feeling over negative emotions, we're building up energy reserves so there's more power available to deflect stress and anxiety.

Breathing patterns influence heart rhythms and vice versa, as the heart is the primary regulator of respiratory rhythm. How does this happen? The answer lies in the experience of positive emotions: sincerely feeling love, care, and appreciation.

We can't teach to others what we don't know ourselves. Rather than just reading the suggestions described below, see if you can fully experience the power of these images:

> *Imagine your breath flowing through your heart. Imagine the warmth of the breath warming your heart. Now imagine feeling grateful for someone in your life or appreciative of something. (Alternately, recall a positive, fun feeling or time and reexperience that feeling at this moment.) Become aware of a warm, melting sensation right in the center of your chest.*

Up until now we've focused on combining slow abdominal breathing with creative imagery, but this process can't just be an exercise in mental visualization. The associated positive emotion is the crucial ingredient that calms the mind. The mind doesn't calm the mind, the heart does. Instead of trying to be still and make the mind go blank, focus on the heart as if it were the center of your being.

Purposely slowing down your breathing can be a good place to begin. Focus on slowing your breath to about six breaths per minute or ten seconds per breath. You can use a clock with a second hand and inhale for five seconds and exhale for five seconds. You could also count 1 one thousand, 2 one thousand, 3 one thousand, 4 one thousand, and 5 one thousand to mark five seconds. If you're comfortable with five seconds in and five seconds breathing out, you can try four seconds to inhale and six seconds to exhale. As you take six breaths per minute, imagine the warmth of the breath warming and soothing your heart.

We associate a warm heart with warm emotions. Feelings of love and gratitude can be love towards family or friends, a pet, yourself, or a love of something greater than yourself. Where your mind travels to when imagining feelings of gratitude doesn't matter as long as positive emotions are being generated. Think of the heart as moving from being a closed fist to an extended open hand. Imagine the heart as big, open, and smiling.

Getting more specific usually creates more intense feelings of love and gratitude. For example, as you imagine warm breath flowing in and out of your heart, imagine the feeling of looking into the eyes of a loved one and having that person look back at you. My heart warms instantly whenever I imagine the smiling faces of my daughters when they were small children. The heart opens when it feels like it could explode from so much love. Similarly, imagine the feeling in your chest when someone gives you a hug, maybe after you've had a fight and forgiven each other, and your heart fills with gratitude. To deepen the experience, try placing your right hand over your heart. Imagine warm feelings radiating in concentric circles from your heart.

If you practice warming your heart in response to everyday annoyances and disappointments, you'll establish a memory bank of success stories: solid evidence that in just a short period of time your physical and emotional state can be dramatically altered. By practicing on petty frustrations, you'll be prepared to breathe into your heart center if panic signals emerge.

In the previous chapter, I recommended the Emwave Personal Stress Reliever as a trainer for finding a slow breath cycle, but that's not why this biofeedback device was developed. The main purpose has to do with increasing heart-rate variability with heartwarming strategies in order to decrease stress and improve both physical and emotional wellbeing. For those who have the financial resources, practicing with the Emwave can be very beneficial because it provides immediate feedback as to whether they've reached the desired state. Some clinicians purchase a number of Emwaves and have them available on a rental basis.

For those who may have difficulty finding appreciation, try beginning with dark humor. What can they find to appreciate when starting to panic? Can they appreciate that the alarm system works? Can they feel grateful to still be standing? Can they marvel at how the mind produces so many thoughts in such a short period of time?

Just encourage feeling gratitude for anything at all, and the heart will know what to do with that emotion. Most cultures or religions have traditions for expressing gratitude for food. One of my favorite restaurants in Los Angeles and San Francisco bears the name Café Gratitude. Each menu item has a self-affirming name such as "I am loved," or "I am fulfilled." Just placing an order provides an opportunity to say something affirming, experience appreciation and warm the heart.

The heart's signals influence those around us. Negativity or fear produces a different signal than appreciation. The resulting energy radiates beyond the physical body. How many times have you felt either comfortable or uneasy around someone but may not have been able to fully articulate why? Have you heard of the expression "giving off negative vibes"? Thoughts and feelings have their own magnetic energy that attracts energy of a similar nature. So negative energy attracts negative energy, and positive energy attracts positive energy. How does this relate to the therapy process? Therapists project their energy, so try warming your heart by finding gratitude the next time you meet with a client.

Parents and children as well as couples can be taught to use heartwarming techniques together. Simply suggest feeling the heart beating, imagining the warmth of the breath flowing through the heart, and feeling love and appreciation for the other person.

Rather than responding with frustration, shame, and guilt, parents can breathe slowly and find gratitude, even when their child is in the middle of a tantrum. Rather than attempting to force a change in behavior, which usually backfires, parents or other caregivers can practice evoking feelings of love and appreciation so as not to drain their own energy reserves. Adults can imagine that the child will feel their positive heart signals. By practicing heartwarming, parents and caregivers can stay balanced and not slip into overcare. Overcare, particularly when it's extended to someone with special needs, often leads to anxiety and fear. Caring intentions should be restorative to both parties involved and not drain energy stores.

Be Prepared: Keep a Full Supply of Images Handy

In this chapter, we looked at the power of positive associations. If you followed along, what was most appealing? Was it going outside to observe nature, coming inside to favorite surroundings, playing with breath or warming the heart? How about some combination? Hopefully you're aware of what images most effectively create positive feelings. Trust that you carry them with you at all times. They're available for your personal use and can be offered to clients.

Even though the best associations occur spontaneously, sometimes tangible reminders are beneficial, so recommend having positive images handy. In the midst of a full-blown panic attack, evoking helpful imagery can be challenging as the symptoms of panic take center stage and it's difficult to focus on anything but the awful feelings of anxiety. I often suggest posting pictures that evoke positive associations in easily accessible locations, such as bathroom mirrors, by the kitchen sink, and on cell phones or screensavers. Some clients benefit from carrying a picture with them combined with a verbal description to be read aloud when they're beginning to feel uncomfortable.

Relaxing images can be prepared in advance, similar to rehearsing a speech. In addition to making a recording of a relaxation exercise, create a slide show of soothing images to be used as a screensaver on a computer. Experiment with developing an appreciation list as entries in a journal, a recording device or even a memo application on a computer or cellular phone. Children like to draw what they're appreciative of, possibly embellished with heart-shaped designs, followed by closing their eyes and picturing the images in their mind's eye.

As your clients practice the techniques described in this book, pretty soon they'll have a very powerful image to use: the memory of stopping panic. They can think back to this experience and remember it when symptoms develop. The memory book will expand as more of these positive experiences are added. For your personal discovery process, recall a time when you were beginning to feel anxious, then became distracted by something good and suddenly realized you were feeling better. What a great story to share with someone else!

Troubleshooting: What Could Go Wrong with Imagery?

Panic sufferers are masters at letting their minds travel to dark, scary places. It's important to maintain awareness that attempts at introducing positive imagery could very likely backfire. Obviously, we don't want to lead a client to places they associate with panic or anxiety. Images should evoke positive emotions. Here are some common pitfalls:

Reliance on Guided Imagery Scripts

When I first started teaching relaxation techniques, I didn't trust my own instincts to improvise in the moment or have enough confidence to trust a client's ability to create their own journey. Therefore, I searched for ready-made scripts. What a mistake!

What may be a relaxing image for one person may evoke negative associations in someone else. We're emphasizing being fully in the moment, which implies letting the imagination go, moving from one image to the next, and trusting our instincts. Reading a script involves predetermination: deciding in advance that this is the right journey for this particular client and deciding to continue with the script for a particular amount of time.

Not Checking Out the Client's Preferences

Picturing a beautiful beach is typically a positive experience. I have a DVD of the prettiest beaches in the world that I often play while patients are engaging in slow abdominal breathing. Imagining lying on the sand feeling the warmth of the sun usually enhances the experience. But what if someone associates sun with skin cancer or heat rash? What if your client is afraid of swimming or being near a large body of water? What if he/she harbors painful memories of a drowning? What if someone simply hates the beach?

Many years ago, I used a premade guided imagery script that took the listener for a ride on a "magic cloud." I noticed the client starting to fidget so I stopped the "journey" and we talked about the experience. She told me that after her child died she pictured her on a cloud. Being guided to this association resulted in agitation and distress. Similarly, caution is advised when encouraging patients to evoke a positive childhood memory. What if painful memories come up instead?

Then there was the time when, as a naïve young therapist, I used a guided imagery script that suggested swimming playfully in a lagoon. I even brought in music to enrich what I believed would be a relaxing experience for a stressed-out gentleman who wanted to learn to relax. Suddenly he burst out laughing. Instead of finding peaceful feelings, he associated the scene with the movie *The Blue Lagoon*, a sappy story of young love starring Brooke Shields.

Wrong Choice of Music

What could be disturbing about incorporating soft, relaxing background music? Plenty! I've had clients who thought the music was too loud, too soft, too "new age," too repetitive, or too anxiety provoking. I've worked with musicians who became tense because they detected imperfections in the recording. I've seen adolescents who prefer to relax to hard rock or rap. So once again, let the client be your guide. Always ask.

Wrong Voice

If you're going to guide someone towards a relaxing state, your voice had better be soothing. I've worked with clients who complained that my voice was too soft and they couldn't hear me, resulting in distress. (It's important to find out in advance if any auditory acuity problems exist.) I've had people tell me that I was speaking too loudly. Often in an attempt to create a soft, relaxing voice therapists will wind up sounding like they're speaking to preschoolers. I often hear this complaint from clients who tried yoga and had a negative experience because the instructor's voice was perceived as having a grating, whispery quality. Some clients relax more to a female as opposed to a male voice, or vice versa. So use the best voice: the client's own inner voice.

Too Much Talking

When I was first starting out, I believed I was not serving my clients well unless I guided them every step of the way. That meant lengthy relaxation sessions with me doing the talking and suggesting one relaxing place after another. Again, clients can discover relaxation if the coach adheres to the "less is more" principle. I was reminded of this recently while doing biofeedback with a young girl. A song that she liked was playing in the background and the computer monitor indicated that she was in a relaxed state. But every time I interjected a reminder to feel the flow of breath or notice warmth, the monitor indicated that she had shifted back to a tense state. So I shut up and let her find a relaxing place as she felt the "good vibes" from the music.

Using Commands Rather Than Suggestions

When introducing images, it's best to avoid direct commands. I never say, "Imagine you're at a beautiful beach." If I know in advance that someone loves walking on the beach, I might say "Maybe picture yourself taking a walk on your favorite beach." But maybe he/she doesn't want to go to the beach today. Therefore, stay as open-ended as possible. Often giving permission to imagine their personal relaxing place works best. Let them fill in the details and enrich the scene. I've had patients tell me that they went to their own relaxing image anyways, choosing to drift away from the guided relaxation path I was attempting to lead them down. Once again, trust your client and allow them to use their imaginations. Along the way, it's fine to remind them that if any images evoke negative memories or associations, abandon them and shift awareness to anything that's positive.

Focusing On the Heart Too Soon

Since panic is frequently associated with a racing, pounding heart, often the mere mention of the word "heart" can lead someone down the path towards a full-blown panic attack. Overly focused on micromanaging physical functions, some panic sufferers may spend a considerable portion of their day listening to their hearts beating or vigilantly watching for chest pains. If this is the case, receiving instructions to focus attention on the beating of the heart or imagine the breath flowing through the heart is the last thing they need. With these folks, stay far away from the body at first. Go to personally relaxing locations associated with happiness, and then gradually move inwards. Perhaps emphasize quieting the skin and extremities first, then teach slow abdominal breathing, and finally move to the heart.

Imagery Just isn't Working

It's not unusual for people with panic disorder to complain about having a poor imagination. Stuck in fearful, negative thoughts and emotions, they refuse to go along with any of your suggestions for generating beneficial imagery. Maybe they're afraid that painful memories will be unleashed, maybe they have a learning disability in nonverbal processing, or maybe they're just prejudging that they're "bad at being creative." In these cases, emphasize how great they are at imagining scary consequences. Try engaging them with a very detailed script that you collaborate on, making sure to concentrate on the sense organ they prefer.

As an alternative, avoid use of the word "imagine" altogether. Instead, simply ask them to think about their day. Even if they experienced a major panic attack, did they also experience even a brief moment of peacefulness or happiness? Did they take a drink of water that quenched their thirst? Did they look out the window and notice anything interesting? This process emphasizes a shift towards rational thinking, the subject of the next chapter.

Summing It All Up

- If you suffer from panic, you have a great imagination and can use it to create a different way of being: letting in something good and letting out what's bad.

- Positive associations that create a relaxation response can be found anywhere: in nature or indoors, in past memories, even in background noises.

- Soothing sensory images increase the benefits of taking slow belly breaths.

- Although the best images emerge on the spot, prepared scripts or pictures are useful focal points.

- Slowing the breath to six per minute, imagining its warmth circulating through the heart, and associating that warmth with warm emotions such as love and gratitude unclenches the heart and breaks the panic cycle.

As you'll see in the next chapter, for cognitive restructuring to be effective, the heart must be engaged. Otherwise, it's just an intellectual exercise, as the mind can't make you relax.

CHAPTER 5

Say Something Rational

Thinking Like a Scientist

"Your life is determined not so much by what
life brings to you as by the attitude you bring to
life; not so much by what happens to you as by
the way your mind looks at what happens."
—*Kahlil Gibran*

Turning attention to breathing while creating soothing imagery
provides a distraction from anxiety-producing thoughts. Quieting the
inner voice or "monkey mind" that talks to us all day long can be
difficult. Max Strom, in his book *A Life Worth Breathing* (Strom 2010),
refers to this constant monologue as a mental storm that needs to
be stilled in order to unify mind and body and free the heart so that
joy and contentment can be experienced. One traditional meditation
practice involves simply observing self-talk as objectively as possible.
This chapter addresses how to directly target and eliminate irrational
thoughts in order to still the mind. I'm going to show you how to
observe, rework, and, most importantly, let go by "lightening up" and
finding humor, as anxiety is both irrational and funny.

I had the great privilege of attending a training workshop with
the late Dr. Albert Ellis, one of the pioneers in cognitive-behavior
therapy (CBT) and the founder of rational-emotive therapy. CBT is an
effective treatment approach for panic, and rational-emotive therapy
works particularly well. Why? Because it's all about changing snakes
to garden hoses: deleting the irrational thoughts that activate the

alarm system and replacing them with rational thoughts that lead to a quieting response.

CBT works, but if you're using thought-changing techniques alone to treat panic, you're stuck in a limited model based on applying an evidence-based treatment for a specific condition. That's similar to giving someone a pill. In addition to guiding someone towards thinking rationally, don't forget about breathing and creative imagery. In subsequent chapters we'll consider how digestion issues, hormonal imbalances, toxic overload, diet and lifestyle factors, including lack of movement, contribute to anxiety. A functional medicine perspective takes into account all of these factors so that the unique individual is treated, not the panic.

As you read about how to use self-talk to produce a quieting response, keep in mind that thinking rationally often isn't enough because it's easy for this process to remain an intellectual exercise. To tame panic, the whole person has to be "in the game." As you personally sample and try on the various thought-changing strategies, do so with mind, body, and soul involved.

To reinforce an integrative model, I don't separate a therapy session into distinct blocks, such as devoting 15 minutes to breathwork, 20 minutes to cognitive therapy and 10 minutes to creative visualization. There's no predetermined lesson plan, no agenda. The client takes the lead. I observe, listen, and provide feedback. While the client is speaking, in addition to listening for and challenging irrational self-talk, I observe the breathing pattern. If I'm directly teaching slow abdominal breathing, I listen for any irrational self-talk that will interfere with relaxation. A trained ear detects the language that leads to panic. Irrational thinking is either totally out of step with reality or consists of unnecessary exaggeration. An explanation of irrational self-talk might begin something like this:

We disturb ourselves from the way we talk to ourselves about our problems, not from the problems themselves. When we were young, we may have been told that if you talked to yourself you were crazy. That's a completely false belief. We talk to ourselves all the time. You're going to learn to talk to yourself rationally, like a scientist.

A simple model for explaining the role of self-talk is Ellis's ABC theory of emotions. A = the events that happen to us, either inside or outside the physical body; B = self-talk, or how we interpret these events; C = the physical, behavioral, or emotional consequences, which result not from A, but from B.

I don't suggest presenting this key tenet of CBT to clients as if you were teaching Psychology 101; trust that as you hear someone's story, there will be plenty of examples of self-destructive language that can serve as teachable moments. Negative self-talk is usually a replay of old scripts we've had all our lives, programming we acquired long ago. Often it's filled with self-defeating lines such as, "I'm not going to be able to do this."

Look for opportunities to reinforce the central theme that disturbances come from the way we talk to ourselves. People don't make us angry. Situations don't make us depressed or fearful. Bodily sensations don't cause panic. The way we think to ourselves about these experiences causes the negative reactions. When someone tells me that a particular event makes them anxious, I explain how that type of thinking is as nutty as thinking that the table over there can get up and take a walk. The event can't get inside your physical body and turn on the stress response.

Play the Detective

Pick any event or situation, either internal or external. Now become consciously aware of "B," the content of your thoughts. What interpretation or mental picture might trigger the alarm system?

A situation that frequently comes to mind is giving a speech in front of a large audience. Did your self-talk include the words "what if" as in "What if I forget what I want to say?" or "What if I start to feel anxious during the talk?" How about "have to" or "must," as in "I have to do a good job" or "I must not embarrass myself?" As we saw in Chapter 2, these words are the "snakes" that turn on the alarm system.

What are some common internal events?

- chest tightness
- heart beating quickly
- dizziness
- sweating
- nausea.

What interpretations or Bs might follow?

- "I'm feeling horrible!"
- "I have to get out of here!"
- "Something is really wrong with me!"
- "I must be having a heart attack!"
- "I'm going to pass out!"

What's the consequence of these interpretations?

- PANIC

We want our clients to become detectives, listening in on their self-talk to discover important clues in the form of thinking errors. Practice identifying the following common reasoning flaws in your own self-talk or dialogue with others:

- *Are you catastrophizing?* The moment you imagine the worst or tell yourself that something is awful, terrible, or horrible, you create a catastrophe. Magnifying, or blowing something up way beyond proportion, is linked to catastrophizing. Keep up this type of crazy self-talk and you're on your way to a panic attack.

- *Are you overgeneralizing?* When you engage in all-or-nothing thinking and see things in black or white categories, you're headed for trouble. Using words such as always or never are examples of this reasoning flaw.

- *Is your mental filter out of whack?* Do you zoom in and stay focused on a single negative detail, dwelling on it exclusively so that your vision of all reality is obscured?

- *Do you minimize or disqualify the positive?* Do you reject positive experiences or sensations by insisting they don't count?

- *Do you jump to conclusions?* This reasoning error involves interpreting events negatively without definite facts to support your conclusion.

- *Are you a mind reader or fortune teller?* If you jump to negative conclusions, you're engaging in mind reading: predicting that situations will turn out badly.

- *Emotional reasoning.* The irrational assumption that your negative emotions reflect reality underlies all of the thinking flaws mentioned above.

For a more in-depth description of reasoning flaws, David Burns's classic self-help book *Feeling Good: The New Mood Therapy* (Burns 1980) and *Mastery of Your Anxiety and Panic* by David Barlow and Michael Craske (1989) are good resources. Another book that I often recommend to clients is Albert Ellis's *How to Stubbornly Refuse to Make Yourself Miserable about Anything* (Ellis 2006).

The Power of Words

Irrational thoughts typically contain specific buzzwords. Search for them. Sometimes the mind races so quickly that these "hot" words are difficult to catch. Sometimes they aren't clearly articulated but are embedded in mental images. Do any of the following figure prominently in your inner monologues?

- Should
- Must
- Have to
- Always
- Never
- Can't
- Nothing

Do you have a strongly held view about how you "should" be or how you "should" or "shouldn't" feel?

- "I shouldn't be feeling this way."
- "I should be comfortable and panic-free at all times."
- "I should be able to control these panicky feelings."

What may underlie these statements is the irrational premise: "I must be in control at all times." The need to be in control requires an extreme amount of effort and energy. Because it's such hard work to maintain this state, the stress response may be in overdrive.

Are you detecting a lot of "always" or "nevers?"

- "I'll never be able to change."
- "I always get nervous in these situations."

What's the impact of "can't?"

- "I can't stand feeling this way."

- "I can't breathe with my belly."
- "I can't relax."
- "You can't help me."

What about the power of "nothing?"

- "Nothing will stop these panic attacks."
- "Nothing is helping."
- "There's nothing I can do that will help when I'm in full-blown panic mode."

Become a Scientist

Thinking scientifically means challenging and disputing irrational thinking. By attacking the "hot words" you introduce realistic thinking that substitutes for irrational thoughts. We can replace the negative mind chatter with more positive ideas overcome fears by challenging irrational beliefs.

"It's No Big Deal!"

Watch for the tendency to turn everything into a "big deal." Many situations that seem to be very important at the time they are happening are no big deal the next day or the following week. Are you upset today about something that will be soon forgotten?

- Can you remember what you worried about in high school?
- Do you have a memory of fretting over a particular grade on a test?
- Can you recall the times you panicked about being late for an appointment?
- Can you remember panicking because you misplaced or lost something?
- Do you remember feeling upset because you damaged your car?

How much effect have these incidents really had on your life?

"So What If..."

If I had to chose one technique for quieting the mind, turning "what if's" into "so what if's" wins hands down. "What if?" implies trying to predict and therefore control an impending catastrophe. Saying "So what if?" implies giving up the mental picture of future doom and gloom, and therein resides the power of this statement.

Catching "what if's" and adding a "so" is simple but effective. For example, you might begin with everyday occurrences, such as "So what if I'm late? It happened before and it turned out to be no big deal." Then progress to more important issues, such as "So what if I fail this test? I'll survive" or "So what if I screw up this speech?" Challenge your typical response to physical symptoms by saying, "So what if my heart's beating fast?" or "So what if I'm sweating?" Finally, work your way up to saying, "So what if I have a panic attack? I won't die from it or go crazy."

Practice turning these catastrophic questions into "so what if's":

- "What if I start to shake?"
- "What if I get anxious and start to panic while giving a speech?"
- "What if I feel a panic attack coming on while attending a meeting?"
- "What if I choose to leave?"
- "What if someone notices that I'm leaving?"
- "What if I start to panic and I'm alone in the house?"
- "What if I get scared while driving?"
- "What if they criticize me?"
- "What if I'm away from home and I feel sick?"
- "What if I'm alone and scared and it's the middle of the night?"
- "What if I get anxious while sitting in a theatre?"
- "What if I can't stop my child from having a panic attack in a public place?"
- "What if I can't help this patient?"
- "What if my supervisor doesn't like my work?"
- "What if I can't change?"
- "What if my panic upsets others?"
- "What if my kids see me having a panic attack?"
- "What if someone says something that upsets me?"
- "What if I have a setback?"
- "What if I need medication?"
- "What if I never overcome panic?"

By putting a "so" in front you're imagining coping with a future scary possibility and quieting the mind, which turns off the alarm system in that present moment. Additionally, you're rehearsing a coping strategy if the scenario you're saying "what if?" about were actually to occur at some point in the future. That's what makes this strategy so effective.

Add a Back-Up Plan to the "So What If"

What's more anxiety relieving than picturing a "way out"? Say to yourself, "So what if... I can always..." I often feel anxious in anticipation of driving on an expressway late at night or during a heavy rain or snowstorm. So I plan an escape route in advance. I picture choosing to take an alternate route for the entire trip, imagine getting off the highway and switching to a different road, imagine pulling over, and, most importantly, imagine taking these actions without rating myself a failure for choosing a different path. Just thinking of an escape route is enough to prevent worrisome thoughts from getting out of control.

Medication can be another planned escape route. Many people experience a sense of safety just knowing that they have a pill in their pocket or purse. Maybe it stays there for years, but just knowing that help is at hand prevents a panic episode.

Find Positive "What If's" for a Change

We're so accustomed to the negative "what if's," how about finding positive "what if's"?

- "What if I become relaxed?"
- "What if belly breathing stops a panic attack?"
- "What if I take a chance?"
- "What if I feel better?"

Imagine Coping with the Worst

Panic sufferers have no problem imagining the worst; they do that all the time. The next step is adding a coping resource. Pick any fear-producing situation or remember a time when you had a panic attack. Notice how you feel while doing this. Imagine, as vividly as you can, how you would tolerate the fear and the physical sensations that accompany it. Saying "not a big deal" and really meaning it entails imagining the worst and imagining coping with it, maybe even enjoying the outcome. Practice by extending the consequences of being late to the worst possible scenario:

> *Imagine you're late for an important work meeting because you're stuck in traffic. What's the worst thing that can happen? Maybe your supervisor will notice. What's the worst that can happen then? Maybe you'll get a bad review. What's the worst that can happen from a negative review? Maybe you'll be fired. Okay, imagine that. What's the worst thing that can happen if you lose your job? That would be bad, but would it be life-threatening? Is it possible that getting fired could even lead to a better future? Have you ever heard of anyone who suffered a major setback but ended up making positive life changes? Now go back to the realistic consequences of being late. What are the odds that it's "not a big deal"?*

We want to think like a scientist who is performing an experiment free from bias. On *Star Trek*, a television show popular in the 1960s, Mr. Spock, one of the principal characters, was completely rational because he came from another planet. Our human brain is critical, judgmental, and anything but objective. To counter the fear-producing inner voice, we want to grow a scientific mind, becoming more like Mr. Spock.

Barlow and Craske (1989), in *Mastery of Your Anxiety and Panic*, talk about prediction testing, a panic-reducing strategy based on the realization that thoughts and interpretations are guesses, not scientific facts. Our beliefs represent one of several possible hypotheses and tend to be biased. Try this prediction-testing exercise: think of five things you worried about in the past week. How many actually happened?

Is It Fact or Fiction?

To effectively refute unscientific thinking, clear, single-sentence challenges are effective. On *Dragnet*, a television program that aired in the 1950s, Sergeant Joe Friday famously told his witnesses, "Just the facts, ma'am." Are any of the following catastrophic declarations actually facts?

- "I can't stand it."
- "I'm going to fail."
- "I'll never get over this."
- "I can't relax."

WILL IT HOLD UP IN A COURT OF LAW? OR WHERE IS THE EVIDENCE?

When I hear irrational statements, I often ask clients to imagine they're on a witness stand. Would this statement hold up in a courtroom or would it be dismissed as conjecture? Do the facts of the situation back up what you think? Where is the evidence, the cold, hard indisputable facts? Can you find an alternative view? Find as many alternatives as you can. When you consider the facts objectively, which alternative is most likely to be correct? There are many different ways to look at any experience. How else can you interpret what is happening? The process might look something like this:

Where's the proof that these physical sensations mean you're having a heart attack? Okay, so you have chest pain. What else could be causing that? Can chest pain come from tightening your muscles? Can chest pain indicate muscle soreness? Is it possible that you tightened up due to anxiety and interpreted the resulting chest pains as a sure sign of a heart attack?

Where's the evidence that you can't relax? How do you know that? Are you 100 percent certain? Have you ever learned something in the past? Did you learn to read? Did you learn to swim or ride a bike, perhaps? Did you conclude beforehand that you couldn't master these skills? Is it possible that your body knows how to relax but your interfering mind gets in the way? Does thinking this way help or hurt you?"

IS IT HAPPENING RIGHT NOW? OR WHAT TENSE ARE YOU IN?

Anxiety thoughts falsely assume something about the future, while fear of what might imminently occur defines a panic response. Stopping panic and quieting an anxious mind means stepping out of the time machine and returning to the present. Knowing a future outcome in advance requires the magic powers of a fortune teller. Upon hearing about future predictions of failure or panic, I often respond by saying the following:

Wow, you're so skilled at seeing into the future, maybe you have super powers the rest of us mere mortals don't possess. With this ability to know what will happen next, you could be making millions in the stock market or betting in Las Vegas.

Easing the mind means deleting the "what might be" prediction. "The future isn't here yet, so let's focus awareness on 'what is.' Where's the evidence that something bad is happening at this very moment in time?"

What's the best way to stay anchored in the present moment? Come back to your breath.

Getting Comfortable with Your Body

They're Just Sensations

If someone is prone to panic, they're probably tuning in to physical sensations much more than their calm and carefree friend or colleague. Imagine two people who are tired after a long day and are standing in a hot, crowded room. They both feel warm and begin to sweat. The first woman says to herself, "It's hot in here; I'm tired from a long day; I'll feel better when I step outside or get some rest." The other says to herself, "I'm not feeling well; I'm sweating; it's getting difficult to breathe; I feel as if I could pass out; what if I faint?" The second example, of course, exemplifies the self-talk of someone on her way to a panic attack. What's the difference? The first person observed the uncomfortable sensations, but interpreted them as normal and temporary. Although in reality, harmless fluctuations occur for many reasons, such as changes in hormonal levels or biological rhythms, panic sufferers forget that their sensations are perfectly normal. It's important to remind clients that given their sensitivity to panic-related sensations, it's more likely that they'll notice normal fluctuations that would otherwise go unnoticed and proceed to scare themselves over these sensations.

What normal sensations might be misinterpreted?

- Breathlessness from physical exercise.
- Increased heart rate from physical exercise.
- Nausea from overeating.
- Fullness or bloating from eating heavy, rich foods.
- Reaction to consuming alcohol.
- Feeling hot from the sun.
- Fatigue.
- Hunger.
- Thirst.
- Tension due to frustration, anger or other strong emotions.
- Fullness before a bowel movement.

- Muscle tension.
- Sweating.

As you read the following scenario, how many normal physical sensations can you identify? How could a panic attack have been averted?

You're new to exercise but finally make it to the gym to use the treadmill. You had a large dinner, drank alcohol, and ate some sweets just before going to bed the night before. Before heading out the door, you quickly eat a fat-free muffin.

You realize that you forgot to bring water. You have to wait for a treadmill, which stirs up frustration because you only have a limited amount of time before needing to get to work.

You feel resentment because this gym doesn't have enough treadmills. You finally find a free treadmill, but because you're pressed for time you set the speed at a faster pace than you're used to. A few minutes into the workout you start to sweat and notice your heart is beating faster. The heart-rate monitor tells you that you're way over the maximum optimum heart rate for your age bracket. You also notice that you feel nauseous and have a stomachache. Now you're having difficulty breathing. In full panic mode, you stop the treadmill and consider going straight to the emergency room.

A huge step in conquering panic is accepting bodily sensations as they are, without interpreting them as dangerous or leading to a serious condition. Having sensations doesn't necessarily mean panic or anxiety. The sensations may be indicative of a high level of arousal due to exercising, producing negative emotions, digesting food, or working hard to fight off a cold. Sometimes the brain must work hard to stay focused and pay attention or to keep impulses at bay. For this reason, individuals diagnosed with attention deficit hyperactivity disorder may be more prone to panic attacks.

But I Panic in the Middle of the Night

Maybe you've developed a nice treatment plan consisting of CBT, breath training and use of imagery. Then just as you think a client is progressing nicely, he informs you that his panic attacks can't be related to thoughts or breathing patterns, because he wakes up in the middle of the night with panic. So they have to just happen by themselves, right?

Wrong. Although it may appear as though the panic is coming out of nowhere, in fact it's related to subtle cues. Fluctuations in physiological rhythms during the night are perfectly normal. Heart rate and respiration increase at times, especially if you go to bed with a lot on your mind or in an anxious state. If these fluctuations occur with an increase in level of consciousness, such as between sleep stages, then you may awaken with full-blown panic. The technical term is nocturnal panic attack. If you're sensitive to and frightened by sensations, it's understandable that these changes, combined with the disorientation of waking, could lead to a panic reaction. In fact, many people awaken from sleep in a panic.

When Relaxation Leads to Panic

- "But, Doc, relaxation doesn't work for me. It just makes me more anxious."

It's common to experience panic from a relaxed state. Deep relaxation may be a novel experience and letting go may be associated with sudden fear, possibly related to a perceived loss of control. Relaxation often involves body scanning and observing physical sensations, which might not be recognized if attention was focused on thoughts or external events. The mind misinterprets normal bodily sensations that stem from the relaxation response. Once again, fear arises in reaction to a reasoning error, in this instance jumping to false conclusions about feelings associated with letting go.

Practice, But Expect to Do So Imperfectly

Consider the mind to be like putty. Now picture that putty being reshaped as you practice changing irrational thoughts to rational ones. There's exciting new evidence that patterns of thinking actually change brain structure and function. I heard Dr. Andrew Weil speak on this topic as part of his opening address at the 2010 Integrative Mental Health Conference (Weil 2010).

By practicing new learning over and over again, the body changes and the mind responds. Of all the many complex tasks you mastered, weren't they all done badly at first? Even when you noticed some improvement, you still made mistakes, but they occurred less frequently because you kept practicing. Mastery comes through practice. In *Outliers* (Gladwell 2008), author Malcolm Gladwell talks about needing 10,000 hours of practice before true mastery can be attained. Performing badly is okay, so just start collecting those practice hours. Begin by taking a chance. What opportunities exist to practice coping with fears? I like to think of practicing as falling into two general categories. The first is rehearsal. The second is using the actual "performance" as practice time.

Rehearse… Then Rehearse Some More

Theatre companies wouldn't consider mounting a production without scheduling rehearsals. Olympic athletes train for the big event. Medical students practice on cadavers; law students rehearse in moot courts. Police and fire departments rehearse for emergencies. Their skills are reinforced through practice. How can rehearsal work for panic? Just like getting ready for a performance, you're programming yourself now to be relaxed later. It can also be thought of as giving yourself a stress inoculation.

After receiving a vaccine inoculation, the body produces antibodies to prevent a disease. Stress inoculation, based on the work of Donald Michenbaum, works the same way, as it involves preparation for coping with impending danger (Michenbaum 1977). A moderate amount of anxiety results from imagining a stressful situation. By imagining the situation over and over again, the anxiety gradually lessens. By rehearsing the dreaded event so often, you become familiar with it and rob it of its danger.

But isn't the problem imagining stressful events? Aren't panic sufferers already skilled at doing this?

Panic sufferers may be masters at anticipating and reliving the scary situation, but they're focusing on the negative. With stress inoculation, we're imagining the dreaded event and simultaneously rehearsing coping skills. We're throwing out the old script and rehearsing a new version. The new script is filled with rational self-statements combined with positive imagery and slow, steady breathing. Practicing these new skills as soon as early warning signs are perceived can prevent the full onset of panic.

Another aspect of stress inoculation involves applying new coping skills to a graded series of imaginary and real stress situations. This approach is based on the pioneering work of Seymour Epstein (1967), who emphasized the importance of self-pacing and exposure to small doses of threat in order to overcome fear when faced with extremely stressful situations. In the graduated practice phase of stress inoculation, the client engages in role-playing exercises and receives homework assignments involving real-life exposures that become increasingly demanding.

It may seem unnatural and forced to search for your thoughts, challenge them, and then find a rational alternative. You're learning a new skill, and just as with breathing and the use of imagery, as you practice you'll soon become a pro. As an added bonus, you'll be able to easily recognize irrational thoughts in others. Set an intention to listen for your own irrational self-talk and practice finding your rational voice. Encourage your clients to do likewise wherever they are, whatever they're doing, and pretty soon they'll be thinking like scientists.

Suggest the development of a simple monologue to be memorized while rehearsing. It can go something like this:

- "I'm going to be fine."
- "I've succeeded with this before."
- "Soon it will be over."
- "If I get anxious, it's a cue to find my breath."
- "It's just a sensation."
- "I can patiently wait for my body to relax."

Try enhancing stress inoculation by encouraging contingency plans. Imagine going to a performance but you're afraid you'll have a panic episode while trapped in the middle of the row. Rehearse with imagery, breathing and self-talk. Add the back-up plan, "I can leave" to the self-talk and imagery. This may bring up the objection, "But what if I can't leave?" or "It would be too embarrassing." Respond by emphasizing that this situation presents a perfect opportunity to practice letting go of embarrassment or shame. "What's the worst that would happen if you left your seat?" "Have you ever been at a theatre, church, sports stadium, and noticed someone leave their seat? How many reasons could you think of as to why he left? Did you pay more than passing attention?"

Isn't psychotherapy, counseling or coaching a rehearsal process? View your role as the educator, the trainer, the cheerleader, and the coach. Rather than serving as a shadowy figure for transference wishes, the therapist plays the active role of explaining, demonstrating, and encouraging. I don't present myself as someone who is immune to anxiety. Instead, I discuss my own history of panic and say that I don't teach any coping strategies I haven't tried myself.

Be creative, set an example, and encourage clients to combine their imaginations with their rational voices as they rehearse for the live performance. Rehearsal is powerful: it boosts self-confidence, offers hope, and increases perceived sense of control. By counteracting feelings of helplessness, a successful practice run promotes the expectation that positive change is possible.

Panic: An Opportunity to Practice

Since childhood, my eldest daughter has performed in many theatrical productions, so I'm familiar with tales of opening night jitters, a common occurrence amongst actors. "What if I forget my lines?" "What if I trip?" "What if I get a bad review from the critics?" What's one way to overcome these fears? Professional actors imagine that important opening night performance where the press is in full attendance as another rehearsal, just one more opportunity to practice.

If you've rehearsed via stress inoculation, then a panic episode is "show time." Opening night has arrived, but go on stage and pretend you're still in rehearsal. Symptoms are developing right now, so use this opportunity to practice what you've learned. What can you say to yourself when the scary feelings begin to emerge?

Affirmations

Affirmations are strong statements that "make firm" the positive message you've been practicing. They can be woven into an inner monologue, spoken out loud, written down or even sung. Emphasize pairing them with breath and imagery.

Consider the power of these positive self-statements:

- "I can cope with these feelings."
- "I've been here before and I got through it."
- "I've lived through panic before."
- "I'm uncomfortable but not dying."
- "I'm going to stay here no matter how I feel."
- "Slowly my body is learning to relax."
- "I'm moving forward."
- "This isn't the worst that could happen."

- "I can control my fear."
- "I can control my fear by controlling my ideas."
- "I'll just take my time and practice relaxing."
- "Just breathe slowly through my belly."
- "There's an end to it."
- "It's just adrenaline and my body will soon absorb it."
- "Keep my mind on right now."
- "I've survived this and worse before."
- "This too will pass."
- "I'm still standing!"

I used to think that the best monologue was a variation of the following: "It's just panic. I'll breathe and wait for it to go away," but I recently learned of an even better one courtesy of a three-year-old little girl. While at a playground, she ran smack into a slide, bumped her forehead and began to cry. Her nanny asked if she wanted to go home or at least sit down to rest on a bench, but she responded with the following affirmations: "It's already getting better! I want to keep playing! It's already getting better!" Remember these words of wisdom the next time you start to feel panicky.

Establishing a Memory Bank

Suppose you've been teaching someone how to stop a panic attack and she reports a successful experience. This calls for a celebration. If you're familiar with the musical *My Fair Lady*, which was adapted from the play *Pygmalion* by George Bernard Shaw, Professor Higgins, Colonel Pickering, and Eliza dance and sing the first time Eliza utters a sentence with the correct inflection. Your client has been working just as hard at overcoming panic as Eliza worked at mastering the English language. So by all means don't be shy about reinforcing her success. She just created a powerful memory bank that now has one deposit but will soon be filled with many others. Tell her "it's easier from now on" because the hard part has ended. She was able to stop a panic attack. From now on, it's just refining her skills and practicing in different situations. But what about the person who's still struggling with panic?

Getting Comfortable with Panic

When you accept what is, you change. Put another way, when you give up the need to be in control, you take control. Because panic can be scary and uncomfortable, you try hard to prevent it, avoid situations where it might occur, and worry about your ability to cope with it. Let's not forget the self-blame that inevitably develops when you think you've failed at controlling panic, as well as the fear that others will judge you if they know you suffer from panic. When you forgive yourself for having panic attacks, you're accessing a positive emotion, so the heart unclenches and sends a signal to the vagus nerve to activate the parasympathetic response.

Naomi Rachel Remen, who wrote the wonderful book *Kitchen Table Wisdom* (Remen 1996), emphasizes that bravery doesn't mean being unafraid; it means being afraid and doing it anyways. Self-judgment, whether in the form of criticism or approval, can stifle our life force because it encourages constant striving. By giving up judgment about having a panic attack and accepting the accompanying sensations, both mind and body relax. That's when real growth can occur.

What you believe about yourself can hold you hostage. Remen compares a belief to a pair of sunglasses. When you wear a belief and look at life through those lenses, it's hard to recognize that what you see isn't real. She describes one of the greatest revelations in life as the moment you recognize you're wearing glasses. Remove them and you've released yourself from the shackles of faulty beliefs, attitudes, judgment, and shame.

While attending one of Albert Ellis's workshops about rational-emotive therapy, I saw him suddenly stop in the middle of a lecture, sit down, take out his lunch, and proceed to eat it. Although the auditorium was filled with about 500 people, he didn't care. As a diabetic, Dr. Ellis needed to eat at that time. He was famous for saying that "nothing good comes from embarrassment or shame." In fact, it's typically the imperfections that draw others closer to us.

Sometimes becoming comfortable with anxiety means choosing avoidance. As I mentioned in a previous chapter, I'm afraid of going down an escalator in the airport while pulling a heavy suitcase behind me. I could use slow breathing, imagery, and self-talk while practicing each time I travel. But I choose not to. With no self-blame or embarrassment, I search for the nearest elevator. So what if frail 90-year-olds are navigating the escalator with ease? So what if my husband thinks I'm being ridiculous? I know I could overcome this fear if I chose to practice, but for now I'm accepting what is. I haven't mastered my escalator fear…yet.

The Power of "Yet"

The race isn't won or lost until it's over. Judge something before it's finished and you've jumped to an irrational conclusion. Practice adding the word "yet" and you've found your rational voice. Add it to self-assessments and assessments of others: your clients, your family, or your friends. Apply it to a general characteristic, such as "I haven't developed courage…yet." Apply it to a specific situation or skill, such as "I haven't felt relaxed after practicing deep breathing…yet."

Summing It All Up and Putting It Together

When actors rehearse for a musical production, they may break it down into distinct components: first learning the music, then the choreography, and then the spoken dialogue. Ultimately, it all comes together. I approach writing a book, sewing a quilt, or knitting a sweater in a similar fashion, patiently proceeding step by step until all the pieces come together. If you interpret your work with clients as guiding them towards "putting it all together," then you're on the right path.

Here's what's been assembled so far:

- Use breathing techniques in conjunction with directly challenging disturbing thoughts and deleting the judge in your head. By altering your perception, you're not only thinking like a scientist, but altering brain chemicals. Practice putting "so" before the "what if," demand hard proof, and challenge your conclusions by asking, "Where's the evidence?" Think of the worst that could happen and imagine still existing and possibly even enjoying life.

- Create joyful imagery to accompany the newly formulated realistic thinking. See yourself as relaxed and breathe into that vision. Sense warmth flowing through your heart as you awaken love and appreciation and imagine these good feelings being absorbed by every cell. Find a monologue or affirmation that works, perhaps "So what if I panic, I've been here before and survived," or "It's already getting better." Imagine being a warrior. Give yourself a shield while you feel the strength of each breath and say to yourself that you've experienced this strength before. The body knows how to quiet down when the conscious mind steps out of the way. As you wait patiently for the relaxation response to kick in, tell yourself that you're grateful for the panic experience, as it means the flight-or-flight mechanism is working properly and what's more, you've been presented with a great opportunity to practice newfound skills. Above all, laugh at the ridiculousness of what you're worrying about.

CHAPTER 6

Unclench, Straighten Up, and Move Around

"Move and the way will open."
—Zen proverb

Your clients are remembering to breathe, playing with imagery, and starting to change irrational self-talk to realistic thinking. What's missing? Maybe they're still carrying around a lot of physical tension, or perhaps they need to get moving. In this chapter we'll look at ways of moving the body, exploring the benefits of both dynamic and passive movement. My first objective is often to teach clients how to "unclench." As you read through the following discussion and suggestions for letting go of muscle tension, keep in mind the "heal thyself" principle. By identifying your own bracing tendencies and practicing finding physical release, you're already helping others.

Slow Down

Before delving into relaxation through movement, let's look at a common practice that can initiate panic: moving too fast. Are you traveling at a high speed throughout the day? Does rushing lead to racing, which leads to feeling frantic? If you're "running around like a chicken with its head cut-off," what's the message? Mindful movement produces a relaxation response but effort-filled, frantic movements produce stress. Are you talking too fast, eating too fast, or walking too fast to get somewhere? Notice that racing thoughts arise much easier if you're already racing on a physical level. Just as you want to breathe in slow motion, begin to move in slow motion. Experiment with applying the brakes to your rate of speech and walking pace. Maybe you notice that muscles naturally unclench when they're not working so hard.

Unclench: Finding Muscle Release

Muscles brace in preparation for fighting or running away. What happens if there's no real danger but you're thinking about something scary or wondering if you're about to have a panic attack? Those same muscle groups still brace and tense up because "what's real in the mind is real in the body." Your muscles want to protect you from a physical blow. Due to "muscle memory" you may tense up without awareness just by being in the same room with someone you dislike or finding yourself in similar situations or locations where you experienced anxiety in the past.

Letting go of panic involves loosening up. By doing so, it's possible to reach a state of warm wellbeing. Activating the parasympathetic and sympathetic branches of the autonomic nervous system simultaneously can't happen. You're unable to experience wellbeing and anxiety at the same time.

Developing positive body awareness, which leads to letting go, requires recognizing muscle tension. Because most people don't realize that they're chronically bracing, consider awareness the first objective.

Learning to loosen up requires complete attention. That's how your clients will become skilled at muscle relaxation: by paying complete attention during the learning process. Just as you introduced lessons in breathing, imagery, and rational thinking by suggesting remembrance of a time when they learned a new skill, use the same explanation for learning muscle relaxation. Can they identify something that was learned and mastered? Perhaps they learned to play a musical instrument, drive a car, or solve a difficult math problem. Explain that when the mind became totally immersed in the learning process, the body learned and eventually it became easier and easier until it seemed effortless.

If clients ask how this relates to stopping a panic attack, offer the following explanation:

> You can shift attention from complete awareness of the panic symptoms to complete attention to the relaxation process. You're already a master

at paying attention because you've been doing a wonderful job of immersing yourself in panicking. Wouldn't if be nice to focus completely on the opposite feelings? A great way to stop a panic attack is to find a slow belly breath, then, as you continue this breathing pattern, shift your awareness, your complete attention, to the process of physically letting go of muscle tension.

As we saw in the previous chapter, letting go of panic requires clear thinking. Now we're going one step further to link sound reasoning with letting go of physical tension. In his book *Experiences in Visual Thinking*, Robert McKim (1972) describes relaxed attention as thinking with our entire being, our body as well as our brain. When muscles tense, they divert attention, restrict blood circulation, and waste energy. We've already discussed how the mind makes the body tense, but the opposite is also true. When the body is tight, so is the mind.

Whenever you imagine or recall something scary or negative, you tense some muscle somewhere. You may already be skilled at recognizing this phenomenon in your clients. Can you fine-tune your observational skills? Set an intention to notice the muscular sensations that accompany negative thoughts. Observe your personal reactions as well as the bracing tendencies of those around you.

Letting go of muscle tension can be either a dynamic or a passive process. Dynamic relaxation involves some type of movement. Passive relaxation entails letting your muscles go limp by reaching a state of stillness.

Dynamic Muscle Relaxation

While sitting in front of my laptop computer writing these words, I notice neck and shoulder tension. It's been over 30 minutes since I sat down, so movement is called for. I can simply stand up and reach my arms overhead as if trying to touch the ceiling. With that simple movement, I've just engaged in a dynamic relaxation process. To enhance the experience, I can move slowly and with awareness, perhaps reaching one arm and then the other in slow motion, and reminding myself to breathe. Maybe I want to lift my heels and balance on my toes while inhaling. Then I lower my heels and slowly lower my arms, transforming the exhalation into a big sigh. I've just relaxed through movement.

Here are more fast and easy ways to unclench:

- Without hiking up your shoulders, very slowly move your right ear towards your right shoulder on a long exhalation. Then lift your head up very slowly and return to center as you slowly inhale. Repeat on the left side.

- Move your shoulders as far forward as you can while inhaling, then as far upwards towards your ears, then as far down your back as you exhale. Repeat about three times, moving very slowly. Each time you lower your shoulders away from your ears, tell yourself that's where they want to stay. Don't forget to breathe.

- While sitting or standing, turn slowly from your waist and gently look behind you while taking a long, slow exhalation. Inhale as you come to center and twist to the other side. If sitting, place your left hand just above your right knee to deepen the twist to the right and vice versa. These movements are performed in super slow motion to enhance the relaxation effect.

These simple movements are based on the teachings of Dr. Moshe Feldenkreis and described in detail in *Relaxercise* by David and Kaethe Zemach-Bersin and Mark Reese (1990). I've kept this handbook in my office for years and guide clients through many of the exercises. Because the movements are so slow, they're barely detectable and therefore suitable for practicing in public places, such as busy airports, on a plane, while standing in line at the store, or in movie theatres— anywhere that panic is likely to develop.

Progressive Muscle Relaxation

Suppose someone has a hard time unclenching. It's common to hold various muscles in a chronically tense position without awareness. If that's the case, introduce progressive muscle relaxation. Edmund Jacobson, a Chicago physician, wrote *Progressive Relaxation* in 1929. Progressive relaxation is so named because relaxation develops progressively from one muscle group to the next. Rather than letting go instantly, tension gradually disappears, sometimes taking as long as 15 minutes to progressively relax a single body part, such as the right arm. By repeatedly performing this action, the practitioner learns to release muscle tension. According to Jacobson (1929), deep muscle relaxation reduces physiological tension, and anxiety diminishes as a result.

I like to think of progressive muscle relaxation as a discovery process: distinguishing between sensations of tension and relaxation while also observing a tendency to hold the breath while clenching. Knowing what muscles chronically tense up leads to knowledge of where to relax. Jacobson referred to this as "muscle-sense," the sensations that arise when contracting muscles. Recognize the presence of muscle contraction, no matter how slight, and it's possible to relax the muscle completely.

When you relax a particular muscle after purposely tensing, it relaxes in equal proportion to the amount it was tensed. The tighter you tense the muscle, the more it will discharge that tension when you let go. Visualize a pendulum that swings all the way in one direction, then all the way in the other direction when released. A seesaw analogy also works.

PROGRESSIVE RELAXATION FOR BEGINNERS

Progressive relaxation focuses on the large muscle groups first, because they're generally the easiest to control. For maximum effectiveness, target one muscle group at a time while the rest of the body remains relaxed. A good place to begin is with the wrists. As an added bonus, these exercises will ease carpel tunnel syndrome.

Try out the following simple exercises for recognizing tension. If you choose to teach them to clients, emphasize the importance of home practice. The instructions can be written out, or better yet, spoken on a recording device.

Lie on your back with your arms resting at your sides, palms facing down.

Keeping your body still and without moving your arm, bend your right hand back at your wrist as if moving your hand back towards you.

As you hold this position, notice the tension that spreads to your right forearm. It's easy to feel the strain in your wrist when you flex it back, but what about the less obvious strain in your forearm? Can you feel it in the upper part of the forearm?

Does your right forearm feel any different than your left forearm? Maybe you notice a dull sensation. That's muscle tension. You may be tightening muscles in this way all day long and not even realize it.

Now let your right hand rest by your side. How does your right forearm feel now? Do you still experience a dull sensation or does it feel different?

Observe how your right hand feels when you stop flexing it and let it go limp. That's relaxation! Feel the difference between flexing and letting go.

Introduce the following simple progressive relaxation exercises during office sessions to contrast clenched and unclenched; but remember, the key to their effectiveness lies in engaging the mind to study the process. We're teaching mindfulness and present moment body awareness:

Extend your arms straight in front of you and flex your wrists as if pressing against a flat surface. Now straighten your wrists and relax your fingers.

or

With your arms at your sides, make tight fists with both hands. Pretend you're tightly gripping a pencil in each hand. Now release the fists and drop the pencils.

The purpose of those beginning exercises is to recognize the difference between a tense hand/arm and a relaxed one. Now what? You can develop a series of exercises that target the large muscles. For example:

Make a fist and squeeze the muscles in your right arm. Study the tightness and where that sensation travels to, then release and notice the difference. Do the same with the left arm. Then make a fist with both hands, tighten, release, and notice the contrast. Now repeat the process with the lower extremities, beginning by pointing or flexing the right foot, squeezing the leg muscles, and studying the tension compared to the relaxation that's created when the legs soften.

From here, suggest that participants contract both arms and legs at the same time and then let go and notice the difference.

No firm set of rules exists for how to practice. You might go up and down the body, starting from the top of your head on one occasion, or beginning at the tips of your toes another day. Sometimes isolate just one muscle group and that might be sufficient. At other times squeeze from the top of your head down to the toes like a domino effect, then release like a shower of relaxation. Or go the other way. I've practiced while in a yoga inversion such as "legs up the wall," which you'll learn about in Chapter 8, and even while in a headstand.

PROGRESSIVE RELAXATION FOR CHILDREN

When working with children, I tell them to make believe they're stiff toy soldiers, Frankenstein monsters, or robots; then suggest transforming into wet spaghetti, limp rag dolls or floppy stuffed animals. For these images to have maximum impact, it helps to have the actual toys or props on hand. Sometimes I've used the Transformer toy action figures (which begin as ordinary objects or animals and transform into robots) as a starting point for understanding the concept of contrast and transformation. Another association that's been helpful involves The Tin Man from *The Wizard of Oz*. They imagine his stiffness and contract their muscles. Then they imagine getting some oil (omega-3 fish oils, of course!) to release the stiffness. Now all they need is a heart, so we move on to breathing through the heart and finding gratitude.

PROGRESSIVE RELAXATION WITH A SQUEEZE BALL

I have a collection of squeeze balls in my desk drawer and often use them for progressive muscle relaxation. They're inexpensive if ordered in bulk and can easily be found through a computer search.

If you have access to a squeeze ball, try the following experiment: Make a fist and squeeze the ball as hard as you can. Study the tension and where it travels. Now release your grip and notice the difference. Did you hold your breath when you squeezed the ball? Muscle clenching and breath holding go hand in hand. Try inhaling while squeezing the ball and exhaling as it's released. Try alternating between squeezing with the right and left hands. You can also squeeze the ball tightly with both hands. Close your eyes to deepen your concentration. You may be surprised to discover that tightness may progress quite a distance from where it originated.

The children I work with love using a squeeze ball. They pick out a special one and are allowed to take it home. Sometimes they imagine squeezing out the panic or bad feelings. What other images could enrich this process? A six-year-old boy created this effective visualization: fear became black slimy stuff that oozed out of his body and into the ball, which was then tossed as far as he could throw it.

Progressive Relaxation in the Right Places

After learning progressive relaxation of large muscle groups, move awareness to the smaller spaces, particularly the face, neck and shoulders. You can also move right in to the smaller spaces without the introductory activities described above.

If squeezing and releasing lots of muscle groups isn't for you, just focus on one area.

WHAT ARE YOU WEARING ON YOUR FACE?

We live "in our heads" most of the time and as tension is created in the mind, it settles in the face. When exerting a lot of effort, it's common to wear that effort on our faces. We're often unaware of how tense our facial muscles become.

Use the following suggestions as possible exercises in tension release:

Wrinkle your forehead and exaggerate the tightness. Now smooth it out and study any differences you notice.

Tighten your scalp or simply imagine this process if you can't feel any sensation. Now imagine your scalp loosening and relaxing as you feel pressure being released and the creation of more "breathing space." Go even further and as you exhale, feel the air you're exhaling being released from thousands of tiny breathing holes located around your head.

Wrinkle your nose as if "turning up your nose at something you don't like." Then loosen it and notice the contrast.

Tighten your jaw, bite down hard, and press your tongue against the roof of your mouth. Now soften your mouth and observe the contrast as you let your lips part and your tongue move away from the top palate.

SOFTENING THE GAZE

Relaxation of the eyes feels great and prevents the panicky sensations from building up. Going through the following sequences gives your eyes a much-needed break from long stretches of time at the computer or other work during the day.

Squeeze your eyes tightly, then soften them and imagine your eyeballs sinking into their sockets, as if you're creating space between the eyes and eyelids. Soften your eyes more by imagining them sinking even further into their sockets. You might actually feel your eyes move away from the eyelids.

The above suggestion starts with the progressive relaxation method of squeezing the eyes closed and then releasing the tension. However, I prefer eliminating the tightening step and going right to the good part. Try the following and notice how relaxed your face feels afterwards:

Close your eyes and let them sink back into their sockets. Take a big belly breath in and keeping your eyes closed, slowly move your eyes towards the right as you exhale. Take your time, savoring every small movement. Make sure you're not straining by attempting to move too far. Inhale and let the smooth breath take your eyes back to the center. Exhale again as you to go to the other side.

Moving in a circular motion can be added.

Inhale slowly; then exhale the breath while you take your eyes over to the right. Draw a big arc with your eyes to move them up and all the way to the left as you take another big abdominal breath. Now exhale and take your eyes down and all the way to the right. You're making slow circles, inhaling as you go up and exhaling on the way down. When you tire of going in one direction, switch and move the opposite way.

I don't advocate telling someone to stop thinking or let the mind go blank during these movements, as that's a surefire way to increase mental activity and self-judgment. Emphasis is on stilling the eye movements. When you relax your eyes and soften the gaze, the mind gets involved observing that process and ceases to be active.

After doing these simple exercises, notice if your eyes feel calm and rested. Schedule an eye relaxation break between clients or while working at the computer. It's a great way to relax and let go of tension. Remember, relaxation has a domino effect; relax a small space and observe how the good feelings spread out and seep into other areas, affecting not only other parts of the body, but also the mind and the quality of your interactions with the next person you encounter.

If you guide someone else through these movements, use the following line of reasoning:

If your eyes can relax, why not the rest of you? The eyes hold a lot of tension and it's hard to relax them. But you focused your attention on letting go and your eyes softened. You even told me that your face and neck felt relaxed after relaxing the eyes. Wow! What other parts of your body can you purposely relax? And when you relax the body, the mind will follow.

SMILE FROM EAR TO EAR

What's the best way to relieve facial tension? Turn up the corners of your mouth and create a smile. Connect the smile with warmth in your heart.

IT'S ALL IN THE SHOULDERS

Are your shoulders hunched up around your ears? Drop them and the entire body relaxes. Squeeze your shoulders up to your ears; then slowly release them. As your shoulders drop down your back, imagine they're moving as far away from your ears as possible. Women can pretend they're wearing big earrings that they have to make room for. Do this a few times, maybe imagining your shoulders rising and falling like ocean waves. Let your breath rise and fall in the same rhythm, inhaling as you lift your shoulders and exhaling deeply as you relax them down your back.

Incorporate Mini-Massages

If a client associates getting a massage with relaxation, suggest the following:

While enjoying a slow belly breath, enhance that experience by rubbing the tops of your shoulders and bringing warmth to those areas as you release the tightness.

Cross your arms to give yourself a hug. Massage your arms or rub them gently, as if you're soothing someone else.

Rub your hands and feet, even your ears. Turn wringing your hands, a gesture associated with worry, into a massage. Enrich the experience by applying essential oils, particularly lavender.

According to reflexology theory, a 5000-year-old science practiced in Egypt, India, Africa, China, and Japan, massaging points on the hands, feet, and ears reduces stress, eliminates toxins, and stimulates the release of endorphins, while freeing up the flow of energy. Although reflexology charts can be used to identify specific points on the palms and soles of the feet which link to particular organs for maximum stress relief and rejuvenation, using that information may feel like too much work, so just experiment and imagine positive sensations.

Passive Muscle Relaxation

So far, we've primarily addressed muscle relaxation through some type of movement, either super slow moves, contracting and then releasing, or mini-massages. Muscle relaxation can also be achieved through stillness, which is generally referred to as passive relaxation.

Autogenic Phrases

Autogenic training traces its origins to the research in hypnosis conducted by the brain physiologist Oskar Vogt, who during the last decade of the 19th century taught his subjects to put themselves in a hypnotic trance and feel warm and heavy afterwards. The German psychiatrist Johanes Schultz popularized autogenic phrases and Wolfgang Luthe, a colleague of Schultz's, was largely responsible for introducing autogenic training in North America. Relaxation develops as a result of passive concentration, which implies staying alert and observing but letting go of analyzing or manipulating (see Luthe and Schultz 1969).

With autogenic training, as with any mind–body therapy, forcing and trying hard is counterproductive. Just trust your body to do what you're telling it to do. Imagine you're engaging in self-programming.

Try closing your eyes and saying the following phrases six times (but don't fret if you lose count). You can add the word "quiet" one time in-between each phrase.

- My arms and legs are heavy.
- My arms and legs are very warm.
- My heart is beating quietly and strongly.
- It breathes me.

I've taught autogenic training to clients for over 30 years but changed the format and wording quite a bit. I much prefer the modified autogenic phrases adapted by Alyce Green, which includes the mind-quieting statements she developed. Just as food recipes can be altered to suit individual tastes, feel free to adjust, sometimes omitting what doesn't feel right for a particular client, or making up your own phrases on the spot. Of course, the client's own creations are the best. I remember Green at a workshop many years ago relating the story of a young boy who added, "my forehead is smooth" to her protocol. I love this phrase and usually include it in the mix.

ALYCE GREEN'S AUTOGENIC PHRASES

Read each sentence twice, instructing the client to repeat silently:

I feel quite quiet.

I am beginning to feel quite relaxed.

My feet feel heavy and relaxed.

My ankles, my knees and my hips feel heavy, relaxed and comfortable.

My solar plexus, and the whole central portion of my body, feel relaxed and quiet.

My hands, my arms and my shoulders feel heavy, relaxed and comfortable.

My neck, my jaws and my forehead feel relaxed. They feel comfortable and smooth.

My whole body feels quiet, heavy, comfortable and relaxed.

Continue alone for a minute.

* * *

I am quite relaxed.

My arms and hands are heavy and warm.

I feel quite quiet.

My whole body is relaxed and my hands are warm, relaxed and warm.

My hands are warm.

Warmth is flowing into my hands; they are warm.

I can feel the warmth flowing down my arms into my hands.

My hands are warm, relaxed and warm.

Continue alone for a minute.

* * *

My whole body feels quiet, comfortable and relaxed.

My mind is quiet.

I withdraw my thoughts from the surroundings and I feel serene and still.

My thoughts are turned inward and I am at ease.

Deep within my mind I can visualize and experience myself as relaxed, comfortable and still.

I am alert, but in an easy, quiet, inward-turned way.

My mind is calm and quiet.

I feel an inward quietness.

Continue alone for a minute.

(Green and Green 1977, pp.337–338)

Relaxing Every Nook and Cranny

A nice variation of autogenic training involves scanning the body from either the crown of the head down to the toes or up from the toes. Rather than repeating each phrase twice, once is enough.

Turn your attention to the very top of your head.

My scalp is relaxing.

My hair follicles are relaxing.

My forehead is smooth.

The space between my eyebrows is smooth.

My eyelids are becoming heavy.

My cheeks are relaxed.

The edges of my lips are relaxed.

My lips are relaxed.

My teeth, my gums, and my tongue are relaxed.

My throat is relaxed.

My shoulders are loose and relaxed.

My shoulders are moving away from my ears.

My upper arms feel heavy and relaxed.

Heaviness is traveling from my elbow to my forearm.

My wrists are relaxing.

My hands, knuckles, and fingers are relaxing.

The tips of my fingers are relaxing.

The tips of my fingers feel warm and tingly.

My hands and wrists are relaxing even more.

Deeper feelings of relaxation are moving back up through my lower arms, elbows, and upper arms.

My shoulders feel heavy and relaxed.

My chest muscles are loose and relaxed.

*   *   *

Imagine you're traveling further inside your body to soothe and relax your internal organs.

My stomach muscles are relaxing.

My pelvis is relaxing.

My hips are relaxing.

My thighs are relaxing.

My knees are softening.

My lower legs are loose and relaxed.

My ankles are relaxing.

The tops of my feet are relaxing.

My toes are warm and relaxed.

My toes are tingling with warmth.

The backs of my feet are relaxed.

The backs of my ankles are relaxed.

The backs of my lower legs are relaxed.

The backs of my knees are relaxed.

The backs of my thighs are relaxed.

My buttocks are relaxing.

The base of my spine is relaxing.

Warmth is radiating from the base of my spine.

Relaxing warmth is moving up my spine, vertebra by vertebra.

Relaxing warmth is massaging my back muscles.

The back of my neck is softening.

The base of my skull is relaxed.

The back of my head is relaxed.

Relaxation is moving to the top of my head.

My brain is relaxed.

*   *   *

Notice the feelings of relaxation and tell yourself that you can carry these peaceful feelings with you.

Tips for Effectively Incorporating Muscle Relaxation

Maybe you're skeptical about how these long, drawn-out muscle relaxation scripts can possibly be helpful when someone is in full-blown panic mode. Have you ever heard the expression, "an ounce of prevention is worth a pound of cure"? Try releasing physical tension throughout the day and night and you'll be getting a powerful dose of anti-anxiety medication. Initially, practicing may require contraction in order to fully release. But soon you'll notice that a muscle doesn't have to be moved or contracted first in order to progressively relax. At that point, breath and imagery have typically taken over.

For most people, the best time to practice muscle relaxation is when they're not feeling panicky. By choosing a time when they're already calm and quiet, relaxation deepens and grows stronger. The following message may be helpful: "If you practice when you're feeling calm, your brain develops new neural pathways associated with relaxation, so it becomes easier and easier to access these circuits when you start to panic. With practice, muscle relaxation becomes as automatic as the panic response is today. Begin by imagining that this wonderful change will happen. Imagine your brain creating new pathways for calmness."

Blend muscle relaxation into your routine in a variety of ways, ranging from mini-sessions to longer, dedicated blocks of time. As you're reading this sentence, can you turn your attention to a specific muscle group, then squeeze hard and release the tension? I bet that took about five seconds. Any area you focus on is okay. How about curling your toes and then relaxing them? I like to strongly point my toes and then flex them back toward me while pushing out from the heels, a move than brings back good memories of ballet class. Pay attention to the shoulders, which like to creep up to the ears and round forward. Maybe set an alarm to check in with them periodically throughout the day. Many of my clients set the alarm on their cellular phone for this purpose. Putting up Post-it notes may work just as well.

Find muscle release while sitting, standing, or lying down. Practice at work, at school, and at home; practice outside. While most relaxation formats come with instructions to close your eyes, it doesn't matter whether your eyes are open or closed. Obviously relaxing at specific times, such as while driving, requires keeping your eyes wide open. While at home, see what feels better. I've seen some clients relax more with their eyes open. It's even possible to engage in the eye relaxation techniques described earlier with eyes open.

When the alarm clock rings, lift your arms overhead, point your toes and luxuriate in a deep stretch, then release it as you set an intention to bring relaxation into the day ahead. Want to have an easier time falling asleep? Use one of the full-body progressive relaxation or autogenic training scripts when you get into bed.

What if you want something a little more personalized? Consider creating a recording. Years ago I made relaxation scripts using cassette tapes, then I progressed to burning compact discs from MP3 files, now I'm experimenting with using voice memos and recording device applications available on cellular phones. Children like to receive their own personalized CD or DVD. When recording for children, I address them by name throughout the script. As a special project, create a relaxation DVD for a child, incorporating his/her favorite pictures with voice-over instructions for relaxation. This is easier than you might think using movie-making software.

Although many clients ask for premade versions, I encourage them to find their own voice. Suggest that they write out a relaxation script and then read it onto a voice memo or other type of recording device. As an alternative, someone else can be the reader. Making a special movie or voice recording can be great activities to do with children. Remember, there are no rules as to how, when, or where to use them.

Many practitioners and guidebooks recommend practicing a certain amount of time, typically 20 minutes twice a day. While the benefits of regular practice for this amount of time may be huge, I've never been a big fan of imposing structure or rules for relaxation. Most people's lives are ruled by clocks, so I don't tell them to set a timer for 20 minutes to make sure they get in the full amount of relaxation time. Relaxation implies letting go of effort. Trying to relax or setting up certain parameters, such as "I have to relax now because this is the time I've set aside for relaxation" produces tension. I'm coaching clients to use relaxation to let go of demands, obligations, and pressures, including the pressure to relax for a certain amount of time in a prescribed way. I want them to avoid the inevitable disappointment or sense of personal failure that sets in when relaxation goals aren't attainable. Practice muscle relaxation techniques but lose attachment to the outcome. The mind is just observing the process, not judging whether you've produced a deep enough relaxation response.

Here's the bottom line: set an intention to notice muscle tension and release it, experiment with both short and long forms of progressive relaxation and self-programmed phrases, and accept whatever amount of time you direct your attention to it.

Straighten Up: The Power of Good Alignment

Don't fall for the common mistake of interpreting muscle relaxation as rounding the shoulders and collapsing forward or sinking into an easy chair in a slumped position. Neither produces a relaxation effect; instead, they put strain on the body, particularly the shoulders, and make diaphragmatic breathing more difficult. Furthermore, slouching is associated with feeling weak and defeated.

How can good posture have anything to do with stopping a panic attack or lessening anxiety? As you're reading this, hunch over and slouch. Notice how sitting or standing this way lessens the distance between your abdomen and your chest, which makes it harder to take a big belly breath. Now lift your chest by peeling your bottom ribs away from your diaphragm. Pull your shoulders back and feel your torso lifting away from your hips as you inhale deeply. Imagine growing taller. As you straighten up, take a big belly breath again. Notice that you've just created more breathing space.

Keep lifting your lower ribs, lower your shoulders away from your ears, and lift your chest. Imagine feeling powerful. If you're sitting, notice a feeling of being firmly grounded through your hips. Now feel lifted through your upper body and associate this sensation with growing lighter. If you're standing, feel firmly rooted through your feet, like a sturdy tree that has strong roots. No one can knock you over. Now begin to feel light from your hips up to the crown of your head. Imagine a tree with a strong trunk and graceful upper branches. Breathe into this posture.

Keeping the spine straight encourages energy flow and makes it easier to achieve a relaxed state. Standing and sitting tall places the physical body in the best posture for relaxation. Good alignment also encourages mental relaxation and clarity. Integrating postural changes with breathwork and imagery creates powerful sensations. Play with the following suggestions:

- Imagine a string reaching from the top of your head to a point in the ceiling. The string is gently holding you up. Going further, imagine a puppeteer manipulating the string.

- Imagine you're a diva as you feel your torso lifting out of your waist and your spine lengthening.

- Imagine sitting, walking, standing, and breathing in an elegant, regal manner, as if you were a king or queen.

- Pretend your spine is an elegant string of pearls from its base to the back of your neck. Picture the pearls straightening and lengthening as you perform this action with your spine.

- Imagine you're a ballet dancer with a long neck and straight back.

- If you're old enough to remember the actress Audrey Hepburn, pretend your posture resembles hers as you practice becoming taller and lift the crown of your head towards the ceiling. If you don't know what I mean, watch one of her movies, especially *Sabrina* or *Funny Face.*

- Adopt the mantra, "bosoms up," one of my favorite lines from the classic Broadway musical *The Music Man.*

- Stand like a soldier: relaxed, but at attention.

Therapy sessions provide opportunities for exploring both the physical and emotional differences between sitting or standing tall and caving in. After you've increased your own personal awareness of the contrasts between the two postures, advise clients to straighten up whenever they catch themselves slouching and at the first hint of negative sensations or panic symptoms. Notice how simple postural adjustments lead to profound physical and mental changes. Rather than recommending isolated movements, however, we're moving towards integrating good alignment with attention to the breath, positive imagery, rational thinking, and muscle relaxation in order to reach a state of balance and harmony.

Move Around

Now it's time to pick up the pace by adding more intense physical movement. But this doesn't mean adding back effort or judgment. Nor does it require going to the gym or engaging in strenuous exercises. For stress relief, any movement anytime, anywhere, and for any amount of time will do. While writing this book, I rarely sit still. Sometimes I use my laptop while standing up, sometimes I do shoulder rolls or point and flex my toes while typing, sometimes I stand up and get into a yoga pose or jump up and down 50 times (one of the best exercises for bone health). Sometimes I get down on the floor and do some push-ups. Little bursts of movement feel good, but I also make time for longer periods of physical activity to reap the many benefits of sustained exercise.

Exercise to Relax

There's strong and growing evidence suggesting that physical exercise reduces the stress response and significantly improves mood while reducing anxiety and tension. You don't even have to actually exercise to get a small dose of these benefits. Just imagining exercising reduces anxiety.

My objectives for writing this book didn't include providing a scholarly review of research literature. Information about the benefits of exercise and evidence-based recommendations about types of physical activity are widely available. The following is a brief summary of some theories as to why exercise reduces anxiety:

- Exercise fulfills the need to act by fighting or fleeing. In response to intense movement, a message is disseminated that the danger passed, so the alarm system turns off.

- Exercise results in weaker sympathetic activation to everyday stressors because it repeatedly turns on this stress response for physical exertion. Inducing some of the chemical correlates of sympathetic activation improves stress tolerance, as the body gradually adjusts to the physiological consequences of stress.

- Exercise increases the brain's ability to create and utilize serotonin, dopamine, and norepinephrine.

- Exercise stimulates the production of endorphins, the "feel-good" chemicals in the brain. Their release leads to an improved sense of wellbeing.

- Exercise releases built-up frustrations, resulting in a more rapid metabolism of excess adrenaline.

- Exercise increases oxygenation of the blood and, subsequently, the brain and other vital organs due to deeper breathing and increased heart rate.

- Exercise moves nutrients to the cells, enhances energy production, and removes more toxins from the system.
- Exercise improves circulation, digestion, and elimination.
- Exercise reduces skeletal muscle tension.
- Exercise increases body temperature, which leads to a more relaxed state.
- Exercise leads to better sleep quantity and quality.
- Exercise enhances self-efficacy and positive feelings related to achievement, mastery, and control, because it represents taking a risk or overcoming a challenge.
- Exercise distracts from negative thoughts.
- Exercise may include positive interactions if it occurs in a social context.

Imagine if a pill could do all this; it would be a "miracle drug" and become the top-selling medication of all time. Henry Emmons and Rachel Kranz in *The Chemistry of Joy* (Emmons 2006), refer to exercise as "the wonder drug" because it's the best possible way to significantly alter brain chemistry and improve mood. Unfortunately, most professionals who treat panic disorder don't view physical activity as a front-line treatment. Sometimes they may even caution against exercise.

By now, hopefully you're convinced that physical activity can be an effective treatment for anxiety. But what to choose and how to begin?

Are You Having Fun?

Exercise reduces stress, but only if you're engaging in an activity that you actually want to do. How does it feel when you're forced into something? Have you ever started an exercise program or joined a gym with the best of intentions, only to drop out or discontinue? Are you having fun or is it drudgery? Most health professionals just recommend exercise without getting specific. Instead, engage in a partnership with your clients to draw up a specific exercise prescription. Start by brainstorming to find enjoyable physical activities that can be easily incorporated into their daily routine. What activity was fun in the past? Is there a type of exercise they might enjoy that they're interested in learning more about?

As a general rule, the beneficial effects of exercising require engaging in the activity on a regular basis and for a sustained period of time, a minimum of 20 to 30 minutes at a time, two or three times per week. During vigorous exercise, one should be able to talk but not sing. Once again, however, the more that specific rules are imposed, the greater the likelihood that negative thinking in the form of judgment or effort takes over and cancels out the anxiety-reducing benefits. Consider even a few minutes a day of some type of movement an excellent start.

If you find yourself getting sucked into a "one size fits all approach," take a step back and listen to your clients. Would they prefer exercising indoors or outside in fresh air? What memories do they have of school gym classes? Do they like competitive games? Would they enjoy working out with a buddy or by themselves? How about playing with a child? Do they prefer exercising at home in their pajamas? Do they enjoy swimming? Riding a bike? How about joining a bowling league? Have they ever enjoyed any type of dance? Would they be willing to give yoga, taiji or qi gong a try? Whatever time of day they choose is also perfectly fine (with the exception of vigorous aerobic exercise or back-bending postures too close to bedtime). Gently guide them on the journey towards finding joy in movement. Maybe the following specific suggestions will be helpful.

SHAKE IT UP

In progressive relaxation, muscle groups are contracted and then relaxed. There's another way to release muscular tension through exaggeration that may be a lot more fun: wiggling and shaking. David Sobel described this technique in his early 1970s book *An Everyday Guide to Your Health* (Sobel and Hornbacher 1973), but I knew of it in the 1950s; we called it doing the "Hokey Pokey." Dangle your arms at your sides and begin to shake your hands, first one and then the other. Let the shaking travel up your arms. Now shake one leg and then the other. Go further and turn on some music. What you're doing here is taking control of your body by turning a negative, the sensation of shaking uncontrollably, into a positive experience that you have control over. You're substituting a silly experience for the scary one. Exaggerate the shaking so you can control it; then when you purposely stop the shaking, look for a pleasant, tingly sensation to replace the nervous feelings.

Even a short break for physical activity has value. In fact, there's evidence that bursts of intense aerobic activity may have more health benefits than sustained exercise at a slower pace. If you're physically able, break into a brief sprint while walking, even for 20 seconds. Pretend you're running track and nearing the finish line. Not up for such an intense activity? How about dancing around the house? Just turn on some music and dance until the song ends.

PRETEND IT'S RECESS TIME

Did you ever enjoy shooting basketballs? Why not go back to the courts? Even if you don't have access to a ball or hoop, just pretend. Did you like to jump rope or skip? I never travel without a jump rope. Jumping for a few minutes feels exhilarating and as an added bonus, provides reassurance that although the heart pounds in response to the intense exercise, the beats slow down when the movement ends.

How about hula-hooping? It's currently referred to as just "hooping." According to devotees, my daughter included, the circular motions of hooping are relaxing as the hoop itself provides a gentle massage. If you don't own a hula-hoop, imagine having one around your middle and just rotate your hips in a big circle.

What games would be fun to play? Many clients tell me that they enjoy using home video game consoles, such as Wii, which offer a myriad of fitness activities.

WALK

In the next chapter, we'll explore walking as a moving meditation. In *Flow*, Csikszentmihalyi (1990) describes it as a profoundly enjoyable art form. Choose a route, select places to see, develop a specific way to swing your arms and move your body, speed up or slow down whenever you choose to, notice how easily intended distances are covered, and become aware of how many new ideas were generated along the way.

GO TO THE LIFE GYM

Turn everyday chores into exercise. Carrying bags of groceries up flights of stairs, running after kids, vacuuming, or scrubbing bathtubs qualify as valid fitness routines. Try increasing the physical intensity. Can you pick up the pace as you push a grocery cart up and down the aisles of the supermarket? Can you bend and stretch a little more as you do the laundry?

WORK UP A SWEAT DURING THERAPY

Where's it written that therapy must be confined to an office? Why do you need chairs? Therapy can take place in any location, even on a park bench. Weather permitting, I've scheduled walking sessions, gone jogging, and played catch with children. I've stood by their side as clients cautiously stepped onto a treadmill for the first time, and offered encouragement as they found their footing and overcame fear. In the office, I love to sit on balance balls, also referred to as stability or fitness balls, and encourage clients to do so as well. In order to stay upright, the abdominal muscles must be engaged and the chest must stay lifted. Rather that serving as a distraction, maintaining this proper alignment leads to fuller participation in the therapeutic process. Particularly for anyone with low back discomfort, abandon the desk chair and use a ball instead.

Troubleshooting: What Could Go Wrong with Muscle Relaxation?

Despite the best intentions on the part of the therapist, teaching muscle relaxation or recommending movement doesn't necessarily lead to a happy ending. If too many obstacles seem to be getting in the way, let go and find something else from your toolbox. Remember: rather than clinging to your prescription, no matter how beneficial it may be, follow the client's direction. Even if problems or resistances aren't verbalized, gestures and body language provide important clues.

Suppose you've instructed someone to close her eyes and find a comfortable position. Next you intend to go through a progressive relaxation or autogenic training session for about 20 minutes. What could go wrong?

Wrong Setting

Maybe you've attempted to create a quiet environment free of interruptions, disturbances, or outside sounds. That's what clients need in order to relax. Right? Don't all the books on relaxation suggest finding quiet, comfortable surroundings before initiating a relaxation exercise? But in the real world, cell phones ring, walls are paper thin, and conversations take place right outside the door.

What's the response to suggestions such as "my hands are warm" when the room is freezing cold due to lack of heat or too much air-conditioning? As a beginner, I tried to create the perfect setting. Now I welcome any disturbances or conditions that are less than ideal as opportunities to experience the ability to go right back to relaxing. I even suggest practicing in noisy, crowded places, as that's where panic is most likely to occur.

When monitoring the relaxation response via biofeedback, I may point out that in previous sessions any outside disturbance created a shock effect, but now they're in such a state of deep relaxation that interruptions don't even register. Clients who are deeply relaxed often comment that they were completely unaware of phones ringing or hallway conversations. Usually I'm more concerned than they are, due to the old irrational belief that I'm responsible for creating the perfect healing environment.

Not Quite the Response You're Looking For

Maybe the physical setting seems right, but you observe some combination of the following movements:

- wiggling

- shifting positions

- finger tapping

- readjustment of clothing.

Small, unnecessary movements typically suggest uneasiness, discomfort, or that a relaxed state hasn't been reached. Sometimes a different position may be called for. Maybe leaning back in a recliner creates feeling of vulnerability, so I suggest sitting more upright. Sometimes I bring in pillows or bolsters for the lower back. If you notice increased fidgeting toward the end of a relaxation experience, this may be a sign that your client stopped paying attention, got bored, or is wondering when the session will be over. Take these movements as signals to cut the session short.

Instructions to tense a particular muscle or muscle group can easily backfire. Instead of making a fist and then unclenching, fists stay clenched. Similarly, when attempting to crease the forehead in order to eventually smooth it out, the forehead stays furrowed. You want the client to reach a quiet, peaceful state, but now they have a painful muscle cramp brought on by all that tensing. Go back to the basic premise that integrative therapy isn't a "one size fits all approach." Tailor the therapy to fit the client, not the other way around. Progressive relaxation isn't right for everyone. If you want to try it, make sure that your client understands the process, isn't practicing on a full stomach, and is well hydrated to protect against muscle cramps. Always make sure they've uncrossed their arms and legs.

I've worked with anxious elderly clients who misinterpret the instructions and report back that my treatment caused them back pain, cramping, headaches, insomnia, twitching, shaking, or even a panic attack. In these cases, I quickly abandon progressive relaxation. Sometimes they're hard of hearing and only tell me after the relaxation activity is finished that they forgot to put in their hearing aid, didn't hear a word I said, and became more and more perturbed as the session progressed. But their eyes were closed and their bodies still, so all the while I was telling myself that they were reaching a nice relaxed state due to my soothing voice!

For anyone with a history of tension or migraine headaches, I avoid instructions to purposely tense the face, scalp, or neck areas, as sometimes it's difficult to release the tension you've just had them create. Similarly, watch for other contraindications, such as recent injuries, uncontrolled hypertension, or schizophrenia.

Let's not forget about those eager clients who want to earn an A+, so when instructed to tense a particular muscle they overdo it and end up creating more tension due to the intensity of their effort. Although this may be an opportune moment for guiding them towards increased self-awareness, if the intensity results in physical discomfort or pain, I shift to another relaxation method.

At the other end of the spectrum, the relaxation experience associated with letting go may backfire. It's common to fear the sensations associated with relaxation, particularly if chronic muscle bracing feels like a normal state. Panic may develop quickly in response to feelings of lightness, heaviness, or a sense of floating. This calls for education, both before starting a relaxation process and as soon as the client describes feeling anxious. Always provide reminders that these feelings, although perfectly normal, will dissipate with practice.

Feeling self-conscious presents another obstacle. I've had clients tell me that the experience feels weird, strange, or ridiculous. Adolescents in particular feel awkward and self-conscious. Sometimes they break out laughing in the middle of a relaxation session. I love when this happens because laughter is one of the best tension relievers.

Occasionally, the observer effect creates a problem. Maybe rather than relaxing, the client experiences awkwardness because someone is watching them. If we're monitoring the relaxation response with biofeedback, I sometimes leave the room so we can compare what the experience was like both with and without an observer. When working with children and adolescents, parents frequently want to stay and watch. Again, the observer effect may induce anxiety due to a desire to perform well and earn praise.

Here's an even trickier problem that may exist beneath the radar: sexual arousal. What if you think your voice is gentle and soothing, but your client interprets it as sexy? What if instead of relaxing, he/she is getting "turned on"? These feelings are usually difficult to discuss. If you sense attraction becoming an issue, go back to what you learned in Psychotherapy 101 on therapist/client transference issues, switch to someone else's pre-recorded voice, or rely more on relaxation homework.

Often a particular word or phrase leads the client down a negative path. When the use of imagery was discussed in Chapter 4, I talked about the importance of checking out personal preferences; for example, not putting everyone on a beach because hot sun and ocean waves may evoke images of skin cancer or drowning. Similarly, the seemingly innocuous phrase, "my arms and legs are heavy" is definitely the wrong choice of wording if your client struggles with a weight problem and believes her limbs resemble tree trunks. How about "my arms and legs feel warm and relaxed" instead? Although soft belly breathing is a wonderful relaxation technique for most people, I avoid the phrase "soft belly" with someone who associates soft with flabby and overly focuses on obtaining "abs of steel." I may start them out with instructions to feel the relaxation as they exhale and pull their navel to their spine (a directive that's in their comfort zone due to the association with core training) and always clarify any misinterpretation that soft breathing means that abdominal muscles will get out of shape.

By now, hopefully you understand why relying on commercially recorded relaxation tapes, ready-made scripts, or therapist-initiated "lesson plans" might be a recipe for disaster. Instead, let your creativity loose and encourage clients to do the same. Use any obstacles as opportunities to find relaxation. Above all, practice these techniques yourself many times, so that you're aware of the pitfalls as well as the benefits. You can also recruit family and friends to act as your guinea pigs.

Remember that the mind remains merely the observer along for the ride. That means allowing relaxation to develop at its own pace without expecting a particular result or trying to force the development of a peaceful state. For example, finding progressive muscle relaxation may require flexing and releasing several times. Autogenic phrases may need to be repeated over and over again.

Despite the challenges described above, devoting attention to muscle relaxation usually pays off. By focusing on various muscle groups, the mind disengages from the panicky sensations. Here's what's even more exciting: by bringing awareness to each part of the body through slow, deliberate movements, progressive relaxation or the use of autogenic phrases, neural pathways may actually be restructured and new ones emerge.

Resistance to Movement

Start by taking a look at your own beliefs or excuses about not exercising. Do any of the following sound familiar? How would you counter these common objections?

- "I don't have time."
- "I'm too tired."
- "It's boring."
- "It's inconvenient."
- "I'm too old."
- "I'm too overweight and out of shape."
- "I haven't found any activity I like."
- "I hated gym in school."
- "I tried exercise and it didn't work."
- "I'll get too anxious and have a panic attack."

Recommendations usually won't be heeded unless they're specific. Write them down as if you were writing a prescription. In fact, it's a good idea to design a prescription pad for exercise and write down specific plans that you and your client developed together. Include the type of exercise or movement, where it's to be done, for how long a period of time, and how many times per week.

Fears About Movement

My early memories of physical exercise were anything but positive. As a child, I never learned to ride a bike, because just as I was about to push off and pedal, fear made my feet feel the safety of the ground. My experience with learning to swim was just as bad, as I remember clinging to the side of the pool for dear life while everyone around me took off like little tadpoles. It wasn't until high school that I finally gathered up the courage to force myself to let go and float. In gym class, I was the last picked to be on the team, as I was the slowest runner. In college, I never exercised, and met the physical fitness requirement by taking riflery. Fat and out of shape, I joined a gym in my twenties, about a year after I experienced my first major panic attack. So it wasn't a big shock that upon leaving my first aerobics class, with heart pounding, legs shaking, and about to faint, I seriously considered going straight to the emergency room.

What didn't I know then that I know now? For one thing, strenuous physical exercise may trigger the onset of a panic attack due to the rise in blood levels of sodium lactate. I was probably dehydrated; most likely ate a poor-quality breakfast with no protein; or possibly left the house on an empty stomach, because I was still too full from the sugar-laden snack I most certainly indulged in the night before. Once in class, I was probably taking shallow chest breaths or holding my breath upon exertion. I most likely misinterpreted signs of aerobic exertion, such as rapid heartbeat, feeling warm, or sweating as being physically ill. All in all, I reacted to the new experience of exercising by scaring myself. I could have easily reached the irrational conclusion that exercise wasn't for me; that is, it was hopeless. Now I look forward to daily exercise as a source of mental joy and physical bliss.

Putting It All Together

Although it may seem as if I'm presenting a hodgepodge of ideas for relaxation, I want to emphasize again the importance of putting them all together—linking breath with positive imagery, rational thoughts, muscle relaxation, and movement. That's how to stop a panic attack. We're not looking to any of these strategies as the one magic pill. So how would you integrate what we've discussed so far when anxiety rapidly escalates into full-blown panic? The inner monologue might sound something like this:

> So what if I'm starting to feel uncomfortable? I've been here before. I'll get through this with the tools I've learned to use. What a great opportunity to practice relaxation! Where's my breath? I feel my belly breathing for me. I can always leave the room. So what if my heart is racing. That's just the alarm system working. Why is this happening right now? Never mind that. Who cares why I'm feeling panicky. They're just sensations. Breath will get me through it.

> My breathing is slow and regular. My breath feels soothing. I imagine a shower of relaxation beginning at the crown of my head and slowly moving down to my toes. I imagine how wonderful it would feel if I were getting a massage right now. My legs feel wobbly and my knees feel shaky. I'll really exaggerate and squeeze them tightly. The release felt good.

> Now I feel like squeezing and releasing tension from my arms. But I'm holding my breath. I'll take a breath and feel the strength in my legs as I tighten up again through my kneecaps. I spread my toes and notice I'm still standing. I'm getting through it. I'm exhaling and imagining the bad feelings leaving, flowing out with the stale air and through my pores.

> I'm feeling chest tightness; breathing is hard, but I'm strong and physically well. Nothing horrible is happening right now. At this very moment, I feel my feet firmly planted. I can feel the strength of my legs. I'm imagining growing taller as I feel my spine lengthening.

> Now I can take a deeper breath. I can keep my upper torso lifted. But my shoulders are tight. I can exaggerate the tension and then release it. I'll roll my shoulders all the way forward, up to my ears and as far away from my ears as possible. Wow, that felt nice! I'm breathing relaxation into my shoulders. My shoulders are loose and relaxed.

> I'm straining my neck and my face is a ball of tension. I'm going to imagine my neck moving back in space and softening. I suddenly have an image of the soft neck of a baby. I smile and soften my facial expression. Now I really feel the power of my breath as I push my heart forward and up towards my chin. My heart feels warm. I feel that warmth in the center of

my chest. That reminds me of all the love I feel towards [insert as many names as you wish]. I'll imagine my heart unclenching. That felt good.

This is really working!! I'm grateful that I'm getting through this. I feel my shoulders inching up again, so I slide them down my back and lift my heart more, smiling as I think, "bosoms up."

I've been standing in one place too long. Moving will feel good. I take a breath and sway from side to side and remember how nice it feels to dance. I have an image of dance class and hear the music playing. I feel the strength of my stomach as I lift onto my toes. I exhale as I lower my heels and feel grounded into the earth. I imagine a long neck and begin to tilt my head super slowly to one side and then the other as I feel the warmth of my breath guiding my muscles. This feels great. Warmth is moving down to my fingers and toes.

I take another very slow breath. I'm still breathing. My heartbeat is slow and regular. I feel warmth. I'm softening my gaze. I glance outside the window and see the trees. I'm aware of sunlight. I imagine how nice it would be to take a walk and feel the warmth of the sun. I can hear the wind blowing. I hear the trees rustling. I hear my own breathing. The tension is melting away. I am relaxed. I am relaxed and comfortable. I sense wellbeing.

Have fun role-playing and making up monologues. Notice how the mind drifts and wanders. One technique morphs into another as the flow of energy waxes and wanes. Each opportunity to practice presents unique possibilities and different paths to discover. Sometimes the road leads to more intense movement. Practice in the following manner:

- Pick any physical activity that you enjoy.

- Find a rhythm so that you're inhaling and exhaling in coordination with your movements.

- Notice what images you create to enhance the experience.

- What muscles are bracing unnecessarily to signify too much effort or struggle?

- Are you gritting your teeth, tightening your face, or thrusting your neck too far forward?

- Are your shoulders touching your ears?

- Are your thoughts irrational or judgmental?

Keep practicing until you're ready to guide someone else through the process of relaxing through movement.

CHAPTER 7

Distract Yourself
Getting Lost in the Moment

"All profound distraction opens certain doors."
—*Julio Cortazar,* Around the Day in Eighty Worlds

Every technique for stopping a panic attack can be interpreted as a form of distraction. Draw in a slow deep breath, create a positive image, shift to a rational thought, focus on letting go of muscle tension, or engage in physical movement: they're all diversions from the sensations associated with panic. In this chapter, we'll focus on more ways to distract from panic, ranging from losing oneself in an outside activity or breaking out in laughter to mindfully turning inward and even moving further into the panic through a meditative journey.

Moving into Mindfulness

Did you ever catch yourself reading a paragraph, but your mind was somewhere else? Have you noticed this phenomenon in the middle of a conversation when someone else is talking? Are you thinking about how to respond rather than fully listening and observing? Does your mind wander away during a therapy session? How frequently are you completely present as opposed to considering what helpful suggestion is needed, determining a diagnosis, or questioning whether you can really help this individual?

Attempting to focus attention on an external event when you're anxious or in physical discomfort often fails, because the mind wants to stay with the panic or the pain; therefore, giving someone who's panicking generic advice to "find something that'll distract you" isn't helpful. To become fully distracted implies becoming fully engaged, a process that's often referred to as mindfulness.

Stemming from Buddhist philosophy, mindfulness means getting out of the past or future and completely immersing oneself in the present moment; in other words, being here fully by being completely awake and engaging all the senses. Dr. Jon Kabat-Zinn, founder of the Mindfulness Based Stress Reduction Program at the University of Massachusetts Medical Center, refers to mindfulness as a lens that gathers the scattered energies of the mind and brings them into a sharp focus. By looking through the lens, you can discover an entire new territory and explore it to find inner peace, calmness, and, possibly, deep insight.

Dr. Kabat-Zinn likens mindfulness to the experience of seeing everything as if for the first time. It may be helpful to imagine the feeling of putting on glasses if you're nearsighted, or taking in an experience with a childlike sense of wonder because it's all new. How's this relevant to the treatment of panic? By becoming free of expectations based upon past experiences, you won't become stuck in your own expertise. By cultivating a beginner's mind, you'll no longer judge in advance how you're going to feel, as no moment is identical to any other. Similarly, by abandoning predetermined agendas and giving up striving for results, you accept whatever's occurring in the moment.

Letting go means letting things be and accepting *what is*. Although forsaking goals is a crucial starting point for true healing to take place, this concept can be difficult to understand and accept. Take a moment now to consider a time when a pre-set agenda blocked what could have been a positive experience. Would the outcome have been different if you had let go and accepted "what was" at that particular point in time? Use this memory as a jumping-off point to reflect on how mindfulness can lead to meaningful engagement in your personal life as well as your interactions with clients. Go further and consider how having a beginner's mind can help someone calm down from a panic attack.

You may be thinking that this is nuts. Isn't the goal to calm down, think rationally, and stop a panic attack? Paradoxically, the goal is attained through abandonment of the goal. If you say to yourself, "I'm going to practice breathing to get relaxed," you've introduced the idea of where you should be, which in a subtle way creates pressure to get there. The body interprets this as a demand; thus, a low-level stress reaction is turned on. What happens if you still notice panic symptoms? The critical judge steps in and you're telling yourself that you're "not relaxing the right way." Mindfulness occurs in real time, so the mind becomes distracted from evaluating the past or future. At this point, maybe you're wondering how mindfulness differs from meditation.

Demystifying Meditation

Meditation is simply observing: being mindful for an extended period of time with no set purpose or predetermined agenda. Maybe there was a time in your life, perhaps during childhood or while on vacation, when you did this all the time: lying in the grass and looking up at the sky; sitting on a beach and looking out over the water; reading a book for the sheer pleasure of it. Think of meditation as a continuous stream of focused awareness or observation of something in the here and now.

Most experts are of the opinion that relaxation can be the first step towards meditation and believe that relaxation deepens as a result of meditation, but the two aren't the same. However, expect clients to be confused and curious to know if meditating is the same as practicing mindfulness or doing a relaxation exercise. Attempting to figure it out keeps them "in their heads." Remember the essay format that began with "compare and contrast?" We're not giving a lesson and there's no test or quiz. Don't get stuck trying to intellectually figure out the difference between mindfulness and meditation, or between relaxation and meditation. That's the analytical mind working too hard. Let the thinking brain take a rest and just observe. Cultivating this attitude and modeling it to clients reduces anxiety, both yours and theirs. I prefer not getting stuck in discussions about semantics, and instead reinforce the idea that "it's all good," and it doesn't matter what we call it.

Meditation works; mindfulness works; relaxation works. Trying to explain how they differ can lead to counterproductive thoughts such as "Am I relaxing or is this meditation?" or "I need to move from relaxation to meditating; am I there yet?" If you're going to use the word "meditation," however, myths and fears do need to be addressed.

Meditation is not religion, nor is it connected with any particular philosophy or culture. It's not a form of hypnosis and doesn't turn you into a yogi, a Zen monk or a Buddhist. Meditation doesn't require repeating a mantra, and you don't have to sit cross-legged on the floor with outstretched arms and palms facing up.

Strong research evidence exists linking mindfulness training and meditation to reduction of anxiety and panic. In the 1970s, Herbert Benson wrote *The Relaxation Response* based on his research into transcendental meditation (1975). Benefits included a decrease in heart rate, blood pressure, and metabolic rate, and an increase in hand temperature. Meditating appears to stimulate the left prefrontal cortex, an area of the brain responsible for reduced anxiety and increases in positive emotions. An excellent resource for learning more about mindfulness meditation is Jon Kabat-Zinn's classic book *Full Catastrophe Living* (1990).

Mindfulness implies seeing things as they really are. For a visual meditation, pick any object and study it with complete awareness. A flower, a picture hanging on your wall, a tree, clouds, an object on one's desk, or burning candles are popular objects to observe. Prepare and drink a cup of tea with enhanced awareness. What did you notice that you didn't take the time to see before?

In my experience, clients move more easily into mindful listening than into the visual meditations described above. To engage in a listening meditation, hear the entire range of sounds that surround you. Notice the quiet sounds, the louder ones, the noises, and even the silences. Embrace the sounds around you instead of trying to tune them out. Listen to the floorboards creaking, whispers in the hallway, a clock ticking, the hum of electricity or air-conditioning, the honking of a car's horn. Notice them so deeply that the body "hears" the vibration deep inside. If thoughts come up, refocus on the sounds. Practice in all kinds of places: at your desk, while walking, in a grocery store, while standing in line, while riding on a bus or train, or at an airport. If you can't sleep, practice in the middle of the night. Practice with your eyes open, then shut them and notice the difference.

Meditation simply means bringing your attention to one thing so that you deepen awareness of the present moment. It's also similar to exercising a muscle. With each workout, your practice becomes stronger and more enjoyable. Meditating prevents a panic attack because the mind is too busy focusing on the external environment to direct attention to bodily sensations. Not only can regular practice decrease anxiety on the spot, physiological changes occur even when you're not meditating. Just as runners have a lower heart rate when they're not running, meditators maintain a quieting response throughout the day.

When recommending meditation, emphasize that you don't have to sit cross-legged for hours on end to obtain benefits; even several minutes a day yields good results. Also, stress that it's not about making the mind go blank. Two meditative practices that I particularly enjoy are walking meditations and lovingkindness meditations.

Practicing Meditation

WALKING AS MOVING MEDITATION

Set out for a walk. The location or route is irrelevant. It could be a nature path, a city street, or even an indoor shopping mall. Maybe the meditation is as simple as saying "breathe in, breathe out" with every step you take. Maybe you open your senses to whatever attracts your attention, simply observing and noticing the flow of images, sounds, smells, and feelings. I've often gone on walks with clients and guided them through this process. It's particularly helpful for panic sufferers, as rather than finding stillness and quieting their minds, they typically fill it with chatter and anxiety-producing thoughts when attempting to sit quietly.

LOVINGKINDNESS MEDITATION

A lovingkindness meditation, popularized by Kabat-Zinn, involves consciously invoking feelings of love and kindness. Begin by saying to yourself:

- May I be filled with lovingkindness.
- May I be peaceful and at ease.
- May I be happy.

Proceed to extending warm wishes to someone close to you. Visualize that person as you say to yourself:

- May you be free from suffering.
- May you be happy and at ease.

Picture as many people as you like: immediate family, extended family, friends, acquaintances, and even someone you have a difficult time getting along with or whose presence evokes an anxiety reaction. Feel free to spread feelings of lovingkindness to everyone who is suffering, or to all beings on the planet. Implicit in a lovingkindness practice is the letting go of negative emotions and an acceptance of "what is" at this given moment. On a physical level, this meditation leads to a profound relaxation response. My friend and yoga instructor Zoe Kaufman once based an entire yoga class around a lovingkindness meditation. Each pose became an opportunity to repeat the words described above. Everyone attending the class commented afterwards on how emotionally moving and physically relaxing the experience was.

INTERNAL MEDITATIONS

Distracting attention to avert or bring down a panic episode requires taking control of where you focus your attention. In a lovingkindness meditation, you focus on specific phrases while picturing yourself or someone else. On a walking meditation, you focus awareness on whatever attracts your attention. Letting go of panic may require turning inward and finding positive sensations. Most of the time we're engaged in external activities and are only minimally aware of inner feelings and sensations. When panic develops, we're only aware of scary inner feelings.

During an internal meditation, choose an area of the body and draw your attention there; for example, concentrate on your right thumb. After a while, clients report that they notice a throbbing sensation that they were unaware of before the exercise. They became so involved in focusing on their thumb that they momentarily lost awareness of the tightness in their throat or the pain in their shoulder. A great way to realize the arbitrary nature of where we place our attention, this simple meditation practice leads to an understanding that deep concentration on a neutral physical sensation draws attention away from negative feelings.

Going Further into the Panic

Panic itself can become the object of focused attention. Let go of the need to do anything about anxious feelings or uncomfortable physical sensations; just stay fully aware of them without judgment or self-condemnation. What would happen if you observed and paid close attention to the panic from moment to moment? You won't die from experiencing uncomfortable sensations. By uncritically accepting whatever you're experiencing, the judging mind backs off and the demand to get somewhere else ceases. What's the result? The relaxation response kicks in. It's even possible to laugh at panic as part of being human, a surefire way to eliminate panic. According to Kabat-Zinn, mindfulness results in brief tastes of comfort beneath the anxiety, as panic varies in intensity from one moment to the next. Often comfort is found in the inner core, the stable center. One may also discover that panic, like everything else, is transitory, a temporary negative state similar to boredom or sadness.

Distracting Activities

The journey to becoming comfortable with panic can begin by cultivating mindfulness to the outside world. More simply stated: by engaging in a distracting activity. Most of the time, we're rarely in the present moment. Instead, we're planning for the next day or reviewing something that recently occurred. As you start to practice, keep in mind that mindfulness doesn't require stillness. For example, clap your hands and notice how that brings you into the present tense.

Mindfulness in Everyday Life

Start practicing mindfulness by focusing on repetitive tasks. You can turn a mundane chore where the mind is likely to wander, such as washing the dishes or folding laundry, into a wonderful exercise in experiencing the here and now. How fully can you lose yourself in the observation process? Focus your attention on the action of washing dishes: feel the water, smell the soap, watch the water washing over the dish, notice the movement of your arms as you scrub. Remember, take it all in as if your senses were newly awakened, just as a small child would.

Take a break from reading right now and become fully engaged in something else for a few minutes. After typing this sentence, I picked up a mug and took a sip of green tea. But before drinking, I felt the warmth of the cup in my hands, smelled the aroma of the tea, observed the color, and noticed how the liquid felt in my mouth. The experience can be expanded to include the ritual of preparing tea. Can you visualize transforming what could be just a mindless process into a mindful meditation?

FIND A MEANINGFUL ACTIVITY

The first time I meet a new client, one of the most important questions I ask is "What brings you joy?" Typically, the greater the number and range of responses, the more opportunities that exist for healing.

Write a list of the activities that bring you joy. These are some of my favorites:

Yoga	Swimming
Knitting	Reading novels
Quilting	Watching movies
Crocheting	Gardening
Crossword puzzles	Scrapbooking
Cooking	Sewing
Shopping	Cleaning closets
Musical theatre	

You may be wondering why cleaning closets was placed on my list. The movements involved in sweeping, scrubbing, shedding, or organizing possessions can be extremely therapeutic. Years ago, I worked with an elderly woman with severe panic attacks that couldn't be controlled despite numerous trials of medication. What worked? Whenever she phoned in the middle of a panic episode, I asked her if there was a closet or drawer that needed to be cleaned out. Sure enough, she came to the next session reporting that a miracle had occurred: she got so involved in making decisions about what possessions to keep and what to give away that she forgot all about the panic.

In the above example, cleaning out a closet worked because decision-making was involved. Let's take a closer look at one of my favorite diversions: knitting, an activity that presents so many opportunities for practicing mindfulness that it can be done for hours on end. The soothing, repetitive motion promotes a quieting response, which may help explain its popularity. Here are just some of the distractions that knitting provides: listening to the sound of the clicking needles, sensing the movement of your hands, feeling the texture of the yarn, concentrating on deciphering the written instructions for a particular pattern, looking through books and magazines to find ideas for new projects, and, best of all, taking pride in the finished product. If you're making a garment or blanket for someone special in your life, allow warm emotions to soften your heart as you imagine your connection to that person. Another positive about knitting is the portability factor. Knit during a break at work, on an airplane, in a waiting room, or just keep some needles and yarn handy to pull out whenever the spirit moves you.

Knitting can also lead to wonderful social connections. One of the best parts of my week is the Wednesday morning knitting group. Our group came together about eight years ago, ostensibly just to knit at a local coffee shop, but it quickly became much more than an occasion to knit. We laugh together, gossip, share good news and bad. Some of us no longer even bring knitting projects. Interest in knitting spans the generations and brings them closer together. As with many leisure activities, start by taking a class or searching the internet for patterns, yarns, and instructional videos.

Any hobby presents opportunities for staying fully focused in the present and may offer a social outlet as well. If it's a new interest, that's even better, as the challenge of learning and practicing something you've never done before requires complete attention. When panic develops, activities that require intense focusing work best. That's why solving a math problem, finishing a puzzle or playing a card game are better distractions than just turning on the television. Even an activity as simple as counting the change in your pocket or purse can work as a distraction. Another simple counting action entails counting down from a hundred to one, typically saying the number with each exhalation. Counting backwards by nines is another technique for stopping panic. Then there's the old classic device referred to as "counting sheep" used to induce a sleep state.

Although we discussed the power of movement in the previous chapter, it bears repeating that physical activity works wonders as a distraction from anxiety. Here too, find something that requires focused attention and practice mindfulness. Try relaxing by shooting basketballs or hitting golf balls. I often encourage clients who have good memories of taking ballet or jazz dance lessons as children to try an adult dance class. You need to focus to learn the choreography, and the music provides an added distraction from anxiety.

PREPARING A DISTRACTION IN ADVANCE

In an earlier chapter we discussed the benefits of rehearsing for situations where panic symptoms are likely to develop. Preparing a diversion can be part of this process. Maybe start a list of as many interests or activities as possible that could distract from the panic. What do you want to keep with you? Some people don't leave home without a small journal, a digital game (how about an online game of Scrabble with a friend?) or a deck of cards. Have some of your favorite movies ready to go on a portable viewing device. I typically recommend "movie therapy" for children as a powerful distraction. Try to find those with themes that reinforce ability to display courage or overcome fears.

Going through a box of favorite or sentimental objects can offer a wonderful diversion from negative feelings, so prepare them in advance. Examples include tickets to a concert that brings back fond memories, a souvenir from a trip, children's art projects, or a collection of birthday cards. This is a great activity for children. Have them decorate a special keepsake box and then place special objects inside.

Just as many small children carry around a special blanket or teddy bear to create a sense of safety, adults may find a "security blanket" helpful. There's nothing wrong with carrying around a special object in your pocket or purse, such as a small trinket or shell found on the beach that brings back good memories. A favorite mug or item of clothing can also be a "security blanket." How good does it feel to return home after a stressful day and change into a well-worn pair of "comfy pants?" Wrap yourself in a cozy blanket to enhance the image of being safe and warm. The security blanket I prefer not to be without is my personal yoga mat. My daily practice would be out of sync without its comforting presence beneath my feet.

A pleasant scent can provide a distraction from uncomfortable sensations. Engage your sense of smell with aromatherapy, which involves the use of aromatic oils. It's important to use 100 percent essential oils without added chemicals. Keep some in your purse, your car, your desk drawer, and by your bed. Lavender, chamomile, rose, peppermint, lemon, eucalyptus, and lemongrass are all good choices for promoting a relaxation response. When your great-grandmother went for her "smelling salts" during a panic attack to avert fainting, she was engaging in aromatherapy by sniffing ammonia. Fortunately, smelling salts can be made instead with soothing essential oils. Try making your own sachet: Mix 1 cup Epsom salt with ¼ cup of kosher or sea salt; add 6-8 drops of essential oil, then place on a piece of cheesecloth and secure tightly. Alternately, use as a bath salt. Add an essential oil to a damp washcloth and place it over your eyes, forehead or feet. It can be warm or cold. Lavender would be a particularly relaxing scent to use.

What soothing sounds do you want to bring into your environment? Most people find that music draws them into a relaxed state. If the sound of cascading water would be relaxing, set up a small fountain. How about an aquarium, a diversion that provides something interesting to watch in addition to soft background sounds?

Susan Albers, a psychologist at the Cleveland Clinic, offers many other unique suggestions for finding meaningful and soothing distractions in her book *50 Ways to Soothe Yourself Without Food* (Albers 2009).

Distraction Through Meaningful Social Connections

The distraction potential of the activities described above will most likely be enhanced if pursued with others, rather than in isolation. Go back through your personal list of favorite distractions or reread the ones I suggested and imagine sharing the experience with someone else.

An effective technique for letting go of panic consists of imagining someone comforting you. Is there someone who comforted you in the past? If so, hear their voice soothing you. Clients often comment that they hear the sound of my voice guiding them out of a panic attack.

Choose photos of people who are special to you and make a collage. Keep it on display or if the images are digital, create a slide show as a screen saver for your computer. When I visit hospitalized elderly patients who are anxious and in pain, I ask their relatives if they can bring in a computer filled with photos. Placed at bedside and viewed as a slide show, what better diversion than seeing pictures of children and grandchildren? Some families even find old snapshots and convert them to digital images to create a movie. When a favorite aunt turned 90, I collected family photos from the 1940s and 50s, added recent pictures of grandchildren and extended family, and with big band sounds and Frank Sinatra as background, created a slide show that she watches over and over in her assisted-living facility.

Distraction through humor

> "The arrival in town of a good clown is of
> more benefit to the people than the arrival
> of 20 asses laden with medicine."
> —Thomas Sydenham (1624–1689), English physician
> and founder of modern clinical medicine

Laughing out loud brings a release of tension and offers an escape from physical and emotional suffering. In his pioneering book *Anatomy of an Illness*, Norman Cousins described using humor and laughter to recover from a crippling and painful medical condition that caused severe inflammation of the spine and joints (Cousins 1979). By watching old Marx Brothers movies, he was able to laugh, which acted as an anesthetic that allowed him to sleep without pain. His lab tests revealed a reduced sedimentation rate, a measure of inflammation.

While belly laughing, you exhale more than inhale. If the laugh is big enough, you vigorously exhale by pulling your abdominal muscles to your spine and engaging the diaphragm. More oxygen becomes available for cells and more carbon dioxide releases. Laughing confers some of the same metabolic benefits that moderate physical exercise does and could be considered one of the best aerobic activities, especially for those unable to exercise.

Laughing stimulates the immune system to increase production of white blood cells, which attack infectious invaders. Other benefits include a decrease in blood pressure, heart rate, and respiration rate, and increased muscle relaxation. Laughter triggers a release of endorphins, the chemicals that contribute to improved mood and decreased pain perception, and lead to a decrease in cortisol, the stress hormone secreted by the adrenal glands. Laughing increases energy and stimulates the brain to stay focused, think more clearly, remember more, and solve problems more efficiently. Using humor in stressful situations results in fewer symptoms of fatigue, tension, anger, depression, and confusion. Think of laughter as a much-needed break from stress that gives your body a chance to replenish depleted physical and emotional resources. By laughing, you dissolve distressing emotions, relax, and recharge. Deep belly laughter represents the epitome of "letting go."

It's impossible to feel angry, sad, tense, or anxious while laughing. Even the anticipation of laughing has stress-reducing benefits. By thinking about something funny, you gain a new perspective for interpreting situations in a more realistic and less threatening way. As a result, feelings grow more positive.

Consider the ability to laugh the most powerful survival skill that contributes to emotional hardiness. Because it enhances the sense of being in control and instantaneously wipes fear away, humor reduces anxiety more than other types of distraction. Laughter truly is the best medicine: a wonder drug that feels so great it's habit-forming. If a pharmaceutical company could put it in pill form, it would be the best-selling miracle cure of all time.

Several years ago my younger daughter chose skydiving out of a plane as a rite of passage upon turning 21. (Thankfully I only learned of this adventure once she was safely on solid ground again.) About to jump in tandem, the instructor kept up a nonstop series of jokes, mostly related to "going down together." Laughter quieted the fear response. One more example of laughing in the face of danger comes from another of her recent adventures. (By now, you may have surmised that anxiety isn't always passed on to the next generation.) While hiking in Montana, she and a friend came upon a momma grizzly bear and her cubs taking a nap in the middle of the path. Hikers were trapped on either side of the path, afraid to move in either direction. But fear didn't deter them from cracking jokes, such as "It must be lunch time."

There's no such thing as being unable to laugh. We all have a laughter mechanism. An ancient mode of pre-linguistic vocal communication engaged in by babies, laughter is part of a universal human vocabulary. Unfortunately, as we get older, life becomes more serious, and there may be fewer and fewer opportunities for laughter. But the ability to laugh improves with regular practice. What we lost in the process of growing up can be regained, so that laughing out loud soon becomes a habit.

Clients may be so stuck in their fears, negative emotions, and negative thinking that these states feel normal. Any deviation, such as laughing, may be perceived as outside the norm. Maybe you hear them say that they can't laugh because they're too anxious, under too much pressure, too stressed, or too angry. How can you possibly suggest that they laugh during a panic attack?

Remember the motto "Physician, heal thyself" that we've been stressing throughout this book, and consider whether or not laughter is a habit for you. Do you want to add more laughter to your life? Children laugh numerous times a day. How many times during the day do you break out in laughter? Can you laugh at yourself and abandon self-blame or guilt? Can you take yourself less seriously?

To enhance our partnership, I believe in only recommending strategies to my clients that I've tried myself. With that in mind, I decided to try laughter yoga. Several years ago, while at a conference on integrative mental health sponsored by Dr. Andrew Weil, I had the opportunity to attend a session on laughter therapy led by Gulshan Sethi, M.D. Imagine a roomful of psychiatrists and psychologists up out of their chairs and walking around saying "ha, ha, ha, ho, ho, ho." At first, the exercise seemed forced and we felt self-conscious, but soon spontaneous laughter erupted.

Because endorphins are released and the production of stress hormones turns off, laughter yoga can stop a panic response. Encourage clients to start laughing whenever they feel anxious. If they can't produce a genuine belly laugh, tell them to fake it. That's where laughter yoga comes in handy. Here's a possible script:

Start by imagining yourself laughing.

Take a breath in by pushing out your belly and then exhale by pulling in your belly. As you exhale, say "ha, ha, ha."

That's it! Do it again!

Say "ha, ha, ha" each time you exhale.

Keep repeating this. If you're thinking you sound stupid, that's good. The sillier you feel, the better. Make faces; stomp around. Force yourself to smile.

Now add "ho, ho, ho" as you inhale.

You're faking a laugh, but your physical body is getting into a laughter pose.

You're doing laughter yoga right now.

Ha, ha, ha, ho, ho, ho!

Is there any humor you can find in this situation?

Keep going while you remember a time when you couldn't stop laughing.

Keep repeating while you recall something or someone very funny.

Imagine being tickled.

Imagine a baby or young child squealing with laughter.

Feel the laughter deep inside you.

What if you're not comfortable engaging in a round of "ha, ha, ha, ho, ho, ho's" with your clients? If you accept that it's impossible to genuinely laugh and feel anxious at the same time, keep reinforcing the idea that laughing out loud is one of the most effective ways to relieve anxiety and bring down the mounting symptoms of panic.

Consider deliberate laughter as a form of healthy breathing and view it as overriding the negative scripts that get stuck in your head, even the negative thoughts pertaining to laughing during therapy sessions.
 Suggest accessing the following memories:

Remember a time when you were convulsing with laughter, a time when you laughed until you cried. Were you anxious, panicked or worried at that moment?

Have you ever felt angry or upset and laughing relieved the tension?

Think of a situation that caused great anxiety. Can you look back and find the humor? Better yet, can you imagine you're a stand-up comedian relating the humorous side of a panic attack?

Can you practice laughing at yourself for starting to panic?

Try bringing humor into therapy sessions. Do you laugh with your clients, tell jokes, or bring up funny anecdotes? Do you have a funny poster in your office or funny sayings on your desk? Do you save appropriate cartoons and keep them visible? Are your bookshelves only lined with serious academic volumes or do you include joke books and writings by humorists? Do you mention specific movie comedies to make a point or recommend them for future viewing?

To enhance the use of humor as a distraction from panic, suggest making a list of funny jokes or placing cartoons or funny sayings in handy locations. Become familiar with the writings of popular humorists, so that you can make recommendations to clients. These writers are masters at finding comedy in everyday stressors.

Movies offer countless possibilities for laughter. Start by going online to the American Film Institute's website and getting a list of the Top 100 Funniest Movies. Each generation has their personal favorites. An elderly client may have difficulty finding the humor in a contemporary comedy, but may laugh out loud just thinking about *Some Like It Hot* or *The Odd Couple*. My generation came of age with Woody Allen's comedies or *Monty Python's Flying Circus*. My daughters associate humor with *The 40-Year Old Virgin* or *Bridesmaids*. Laughing at anxiety feels wonderful, and fortunately so many comedies do just that. For starters, rent movies by Woody Allen and Mel Brooks. Who can forget the nervous accountant Leo Bloom having a panic attack in Brooks' *The Producers*? *What About Bob?* and Brooks' *High Anxiety* also poke fun at anxiety.

Let's not forget the power of television. After writing this paragraph, I'm taking a break to watch one of my favorite shows, *Curb Your Enthusiasm*, a series by Larry David, the creator of *Seinfeld*. I laugh just recalling the plots of previous episodes and find myself describing them to clients. Do you have any favorite comedies that evoke spontaneous laughter? Any that might distract a client who's feeling a panic attack coming on?

Although some parents, educators, and health professionals discourage television, or even movie watching by children, the right program or film may be just what's needed to deter or stop an anxiety episode. Find a comedy that works well and stick with it, as children enjoy repeat viewings and may laugh just as hard the twentieth time as the first. Keeping in mind that laughter is the best medicine, don't be afraid to recommend these media.

I find the writings of Dr. Albert Ellis helpful because he presents the principles of cognitive-behavior therapy in a humorous way. For years, I've recommended his classic book *How to Stubbornly Refuse to Make Yourself Miserable About Anything, Yes Anything* (Ellis 2006). I'm fortunate to have in my possession an old cassette tape of Ellis singing lyrics about thinking straight and disturbing ourselves less, set to the tune of popular songs on the recording *A Garland of Rational Songs* (Ellis 1977). Unfortunately, the songbook is out of print and copies are selling online for over $100.

Troubleshooting: What Could Go Wrong with Distraction?

To be meaningfully engaged implies engagement of one's entire being. Attempts to force this process backfire. Again, listen to the client and stay away from predetermined agendas. That's usually when trouble begins. What can go wrong?

Introducing meditation too early in the game stirs up anxiety. Sometimes even using that word creates problems. For those restless individuals with racing minds, sitting in a meditation class can be torturous. Until clients are seasoned relaxed breathers and have some level of comfort with mindfulness, I typically refrain from encouraging seated meditations. Short periods of walking devoted to complete awareness or fully listening to every background sound are better choices.

When recommending involvement in an activity as a way to distract from panic, make sure that engagement doesn't morph into over-engagement. For example, if cleaning a closet is the project of choice, look out for negative assessments as to how much needs to be done or the degree of clutter or dirt that exists. If learning a new skill or hobby seems like a good idea, watch out for irrational thinking about ability to master something new.

Therapists offer possibilities: directions to where the mind can travel in order to find a peaceful place. Some clients love concrete suggestions, including guided meditation journeys and recommendations for specific activities. Others prefer to find their own way and report back to you about the details.

Putting It All Together

Opportunities for meaningful engagement exist everywhere and can be discovered as soon as attention stops wandering to the past or future but comes to rest in the present moment. That's when options for letting go of panic become available. Slow belly breathing is usually the most dependable choice, especially when combined with pleasurable imagery, realistic thinking, heartfelt positive emotions, shedding of muscle tension, and even slow or vigorous movement. If you're deeply involved in creating a relaxed state and observing how the body responds, you've moved into mindfulness. But a "one-size fits all" approach doesn't apply to the treatment of anxiety. For some, looking inside can be too uncomfortable and they resist experiencing everything that comes into their minds. Others, particularly young children or the elderly, may be too distractible, restless, or lack sufficient understanding to become fully engaged in turning inwards. Fortunately, another option exists: moving from the outside in.

Anything that creates a diversion from panic works, including activities that require following directions, social connections, humor, paying attention to surroundings, listening to background noises, and even involvement in mundane chores. As long as negative judgment and too much effort are held at bay, all of the above offer opportunities for moment-by-moment attention to something good…or at least neutral.

Use therapy sessions as a time to practice mindfulness and meaningful engagement. As I've stressed repeatedly, the process can't be one-sided. How many ways can you become more connected and observant? Can you shift back and forth between internal and external awareness? By doing so, you'll become more comfortable and more available to offer support and guidance.

CHAPTER 8

Step Onto Your Mat

Practicing Yoga 24/7

*"Yoga teaches us to cure what need not be
endured and endure what cannot be cured."*
—*B.K.S. Iyengar*

- "I'm not flexible enough."
- "I have a bad back."
- "I have bad knees."
- "I'll go mad having to sit there and say 'om.'"
- "I tried yoga once, but my mind raced too much and I couldn't wait to leave."
- "I'm embarrassed about how I'll look."
- "I'm too old."
- "My panic is too bad."
- "I have to focus on getting well first."
- "I don't have the time."
- "I'm too fat."
- "I'll hurt myself."
- "The classes are too big."
- "It's too expensive."
- "I have no one to go with."

- "I already exercise enough."
- "I take Pilates, aren't I getting the same benefits?"
- "It's too slow-paced for me."
- "It's for old people."
- "I already stretch."
- "I tried it once but was so sore I couldn't move the next day."

I've heard all of the above excuses for not practicing yoga. Hopefully after reading this chapter, you'll be convinced of the benefits, know what styles of yoga and specific poses to recommend, and want to step onto a mat yourself if you're not already a devotee.

Let's begin by demystifying yoga:

- Yoga isn't about flexibility (in fact, flexible people are at greater risk of injury).
- Yoga isn't just stretching; a regular practice builds strength.
- Yoga isn't just a physical exercise routine and isn't the same as Pilates, a system of exercise developed by Joseph Pilates in the early 20th century to develop core strength and flexibility.
- Yoga isn't just for the young and physically fit.
- Yoga isn't limited to a class, but can be practiced anywhere.
- Yoga can be free.
- There are many philosophies and types of yoga.
- Yoga can be beneficial for those with physical limitations.

Imagine walking into a yoga class and observing two people while they practice. One has such perfect-looking poses that she could be on the cover of a yoga magazine, but she's telling herself that she's not doing well compared to others in the room. The other person spends much of the class in child's pose, the resting pose between more difficult postures, but keeps a steady breath pattern and stays focused on feeling good. The first woman reaps none of the true benefits of yoga and risks physical injury. In fact, she isn't really practicing yoga, as her mind and body are disconnected. *Yoga*, a Sanskrit word, means "yoke." The second woman practices like a yogini, a female yoga master, by yoking together, or unifying mind and body.

Most people come to yoga for the physical practice. They want to become stronger, more flexible, find an alternative to another type of exercise, or heal their bodies after an injury. But after a while, they return to their mats because a regular yoga practice profoundly changes their lives.

What's So Good about Yoga?

I have just returned from a yoga class feeling balanced, energized, and aware of a sense of wellbeing. Those 90 minutes of sustained mental presence created more healing than the most powerful medicine. Yoga made such a big difference in my life that I chose to become certified as a yoga instructor a few years ago. When traveling, a yoga mat accompanies me. I attend a class at various yoga studios whenever I can, but also roll out my mat at home.

Coming to a class fosters a sense of community, but yoga need not be restricted to a structured program. My home practice may be 20 minutes to an hour, but sometimes it's just a pose or two as a short break. I start each day with an invigorating inversion and standing pose and end each night with a relaxing seated forward bend. A spare mat stays at my office, and whenever I have 10 to 15 minutes between clients, I close my door, spread out the mat, and find a few poses based on what might feel best at that moment. Since I often want more energy after a long period of sitting, backbends usually fit the bill.

While writing this book, my favorite breaks consist of moving into King Dancer pose (Figure 8.1). I love this pose, because it's an awakening backbend to counterbalance sitting at the computer, a balancing pose that requires slow breathing and concentration, plus it evokes images of gracefulness, hence the name, "King Dancer." Just one pose incorporates movement, balance, strength, breath, imagery, imagination, and mindfulness: everything we've been discussing to calm the mind and quiet the body.

Yoga wasn't always my passion. After years of training in ballet and jazz dance, I assumed that another stretching class would be superfluous, so why bother with yoga? I took one yoga class in the early 1970s and found it boring but chose to try another style about ten years ago. After that first vinyassa flow class (a style of yoga that links breath with a series of movements), I was hooked. This wasn't the yoga practice I remembered! Instead of boring, it felt exhilarating and relaxing at the same time.

Want a surefire way to overcome fears? Try yoga. The first time I attended a class and saw students performing handstands and headstands, I told myself, "I can't do this; I'm too scared; I'm too old; I'll get hurt." But I didn't roll up my mat and go home. Instead, I started where I felt safe and, with the support of a good teacher and hours of practice, took baby steps. I can think of no better example of moving slowly towards mastery, but as in life, it's the journey that matters and not reaching the goal, as another level and more advanced postures always lie ahead.

By regularly practicing yoga, one reaps all the benefits of an energetic physical workout, including increased muscular strength, stamina, sense of balance, and flexibility. Certain styles of yoga can also be an aerobic activity. But these benefits, although significant, can be found by working out at any local·gym and aren't what defines this ancient practice as special. Most importantly, yoga links breath to movement. A moving meditation that connects mind and body, yoga represents the epitome of mindfulness. Moving into a pose, holding a pose, or flowing from one pose to the next, all enhance awareness of the body's internal movements. What's more, they offer opportunities to notice that the changes being created are genuine.

Figure 8.1 King Dancer pose

Regular practice helps to minimize anxiety symptoms. Yoga has been described by Amy Weintraub, author of *Yoga for Depression* (Weintraub 2004), as preventative and positive medicine that quiets the sympathetic branch of the autonomic nervous system. As a direct result of practicing of yoga, cortisol levels decrease, and the vagus nerve, which is responsible for turning on the parasympathetic response, gets activated.

Yoga may alter brain chemistry more directly and efficiently than regular exercise, as it provides the brain with a balance of stimulation and relaxation. Increases in alpha wave activity, the brain wave state associated with relaxation, and theta brain waves, associated with daydreaming and reverie, have been directly tied to yoga. Other physiological changes include elevations of GABA, an inhibitory neurotransmitter, increases in heart-rate variability (linked with heart health and a coherent state), and increased delivery of oxygen and glucose to the brain. As we've seen, anxiety is associated with activation of the sympathetic nervous system, shunting of oxygen away from the higher brain centers, low levels of GABA, and decreased heart-rate variability.

Far from being uniform, styles of yoga differ considerably, ranging from restorative, gentle yin yoga to strength-building power yoga. Classes can be found at the local health club or at dedicated studios. Sometimes the room may be heated for a detoxifying "hot yoga" experience. But although the physical surroundings, choice of specific poses (referred to as *asanas* in Sanskrit), transitions between poses, length of time holding each pose, and total time devoted to the practice vary considerably, the ingredients that make yoga so beneficial hold constant.

Even if you already practice yoga, approach it in a different way; see yourself as a beginning student. Each time you come to the mat, create a good intention or affirmation, find your breath, use positive imagery, let go of judgment and effort, scan the body to release tension, develop greater awareness, practice self-acceptance, and warm the heart with gratitude. The sum total of everything we've covered up until now, the cultivation of grace in uncomfortable situations...that's yoga.

We're All Beginners

I recommend yoga to most everyone who walks in my door, but initially I may avoid any mention of the word "yoga," as the term frequently evokes the negative associations listed at the start of this chapter. Because the most significant feature of yoga lies in the use of breath, I inform clients that they're already doing yoga if they're practicing slow, abdominal breathing.

If you've never practiced yoga, ask yourself if you're intimidated by the thought of being in a class or trying certain poses. Are you unsure of how to recommend yoga or how to incorporate it into a session? If you're an experienced practitioner, did any of the objections or concerns described earlier resonate? You don't need to be a yoga instructor to reinforce a yoga philosophy or suggest some of the poses I'll be taking you through.

As with any recommendation, provide enough details and specifics to facilitate compliance. It's not enough to suggest taking a yoga class. Specifics are required to prevent negative consequences, not only for the client but for you as well. What if a client whose panic attacks are associated with feeling warm chooses a Bikram (hot yoga) class (in which room temperature = 105°F/40.6°C) as her first experience? What if a newcomer attends a class at a local gym and, due to lack of proper guidance, suffers an injury?

If yoga is medicine, then envision prescribing yoga in just as careful a manner as writing a prescription for a drug. Provide all the details; even write them down on a "prescription pad." Know the yoga studios in the area and who teaches in those studios. Just as you wouldn't blindly prescribe a medication or refer a client to another healthcare professional you knew nothing about, don't refer to a yoga program you aren't familiar with. Take a variety of classes yourself and get to know which ones are best to recommend given individual needs and preferences. I like to prescribe specific classes and teachers and hand clients a written sheet with the studio name, the name of the class, and the teacher they should study with.

Assume you've diligently researched local resources for yoga and provided a specific recommendation; the next step involves preparation to ensure a positive experience. Always remind clients that being a beginner is "where they need to be." In fact, a key component of yoga involves cultivating a beginner's mind so as to experience the freedom and joy that comes from staying fully present and maintaining a sense of wonder. Emphasize practicing without striving, effort, or forcing. It's not about doing; it's about just being, which implies accepting the body as is. Staying in the present, maintaining moment-to-moment awareness, yoga is a moving meditation. When practiced this way, the body stays calm and injuries are prevented.

Expect that someone with panic will have an over-stimulated, racing mind, and attempts to quiet it during a yoga practice may only lead to more negative thoughts. Imagine being told to sit in a cross-legged position with your arms resting palms up on your knees, eyes closed. For some, that's the perfect set-up for panic to develop. The quieter the room and the longer the "relaxation/ meditation" continues, the busier the mind gets and the more agitated it becomes. Similarly, *savasana*, the corpse pose that ends every yoga session, also offers an opportunity for panic symptoms to develop. It's not unusual to leave class tenser and fraught with greater turmoil than before starting the session. For these reasons, I may initially prescribe a yoga style that's active, such as a *vinyassa* flow class. By accommodating the anxious state with a vigorous practice, the mind becomes distracted, as concentration is required to learn and execute the poses. Due to meaningful engagement, the mind settles down. In time, quieter poses become easier.

To prevent experiencing panic during a yoga session, suggest that clients make the practice their own. Grant them permission to keep their eyes open and not chant *om* along with everyone else, to move and stretch when instructed to stay still, and even to leave early if feeling anxious. Reinforce the importance of thinking like a beginner by accepting mistakes and moving on. Judith Lassater, author of *Relax and Renew*, refers to yoga as a practice of happiness and suggests saying, "how human of me" while moving through the various poses (Lasater 1995). Why let judgment get in the way? Stepping onto the mat equals a time when the thinking, critical mind takes a rest. Yogis check this part of their brains at the door along with their coats, shoes, cellphones, and watches.

Rather than letting effort and self-evaluation get in the way, remember that "wherever you're at is where you need to be." Yogis "stay on their own mat." One of my teachers likes to say, "Don't do your neighbor's practice." Looking around the room, you can easily identify students who seem more advanced or physically stronger. It's common to feel inadequate and judged, or attempt poses your body isn't designed or ready for just because everyone else in the room seems to be doing them with ease.

Finding the Best Poses

Everyone can practice yoga. They can practice standing up, seated, or lying down. They can practice at home, at work, outside, in bed, and even in a wheelchair. Appropriate poses can be found for the four-year-old and the 94-year-old. The only requirement: inhaling and exhaling breath.

I hope this chapter provides the incentive to create your own home- and office-based practice. In addition to receiving the many benefits, you'll be able to intelligently prescribe it to clients. Learn about the power of yoga by standing up and moving into the following *asanas*. However, by no means are these descriptions meant to be a complete guide to yoga. I've listed some good resources in Appendix 1, but it's hard to learn yoga from a book, a website, or a DVD. Nothing takes the place of going to class and studying with a good teacher. Above all, know your body and move with awareness to avoid injury. If something doesn't feel right, don't do it.

Some Basic Poses

A few basic *asanas* can provide everything you need. Let's start with three: Mountain pose, Cat–Cow sequence, and Child's pose. Mountain pose (Figure 8.2) is all about setting an intention, breathing and finding good alignment. The Cat–Cow sequence (Figures 8.3, 8.4) warms up the spine and engages the belly. The restorative Child's pose (Figures 8.5, 8.6) provides an opportunity to surrender, connect with the earth, and allow it to support you.

MOUNTAIN POSE

All poses are built from the ground up. So begin by planting your feet firmly. Lift and spread all ten toes. Let your feet be parallel to each other and as if they were rectangles, feel all four corners rooted down. Place a little more weight on the balls of your feet than on your heels.

Squeeze your kneecaps and feel the strength and energy in your legs. Imagine you have a block between your inner thighs and you're trying to keep it from falling down. Ever so slightly, the inner thighs will rotate inwardly to grab the block.

Feel the strength of your belly and as you exhale, slightly tuck your tailbone. Now feel your torso lengthening and lift your bottom rib away from your diaphragm. Feel your chest lifting and slide your shoulder blades down your back and away from your ears. With your arms at your sides, turn your palms face up. Let your collarbone stay wide and open. Feel length through the back of your neck. To deepen the experience, close your eyes. With each inhalation, feel yourself growing taller and lengthening both sides of your torso. With each exhalation, breathe into your lower back and feel grounded through your feet.

Figure 8.2 Mountain pose

Feel as solid and steadfast as a mountain as you continue to breathe slowly. Soften your face and let any tension melt away. Due to misplaced effort, we often "wear the pose on our faces." Release the effort and notice the sweetness of the pose. Smile.

Whether you're standing in Mountain pose, balancing on one leg, or standing on your hands in a handstand, the basic alignment that I just described never varies. All poses involve attention to the breath; all are simultaneously relaxing and energizing.

CAT–COW SEQUENCE

As you place your hands and knees on the mat, spread your fingers wide. Glance down and make sure your shoulders are over your wrists and your hips are over your knees. As you inhale, sink your spine between your shoulder blades and draw your chest forward to arch your upper back while lifting your tailbone towards the ceiling. Gently look up without straining your neck. You're now in Cow pose (Figure 8.3).

Figure 8.3 Cow pose

Figure 8.4 Cat pose

As you exhale, draw your navel in and up towards your spine as you begin to round the lower back by curling your tailbone towards you. Imagine the arched body of a cat. Relax your neck and look back at your navel. You are now in Cat pose (Figure 8.4). Continue for a few more breath cycles, imagining your spine becoming warmer.

CHILD'S POSE

Sink your hips toward your heels, keep your arms at your sides, palms up (Figure 8.5) or outstretched in front of you (Figure 8.6). Relax your chin. Breathe slowly as you feel your spine lengthening and melting into the earth.

Figure 8.5 Child's pose I

Figure 8.6 Child's pose II

Developing a Complete Practice

All yoga postures offer opportunities to practice mindfulness. As you lift and lower, twist and turn, you're moving with the breath and paying conscious attention to physical sensations, thoughts, and emotions. A complete practice involves moving the spine forwards, backwards, and sideways, and also includes strengthening poses, twists, balancing postures, and inversions. The practice incorporates standing *asanas* and those performed in a seated or prone position, thus balancing energizing poses with quieting, restorative positions.

Forward bends (e.g. Figure 8.7) calm the nervous system, but if you want an energizing pose, choose a backbend such as Cobra, Bow pose, Bridge, or Camel (Figure 8.8). Make sure you lead from your chest and keep your tailbone gently tucked to protect the lower back. A supported bridge can be a great option if you're new to yoga or have lower back problems. Simply place a block or bolster at your mid-back, open your arms out to the sides and arch your upper back. Back bending feels great after sitting in a hunched over position for long periods of time.

Figure 8.7 Supported seated forward bend

Want to feel strong and invincible? Practice a warrior pose, especially Warrior II (Figure 8.9). Feel firmly grounded in your feet, become aware of the strength in your legs, pull your navel towards your spine with each exhalation, spread your arms like wings, and soften your face. Feel the balance between strength and softness as you maintain a steady breathing pattern for at least five breath cycles.

Figure 8.8 Camel pose   *Figure 8.9 Warrior II pose*

There's nothing like a balancing pose, such as Tree (Figure 8.10), for experiencing a sense of equanimity. Find a gazing point, pour all your weight into one foot, place the other foot on your leg, either above or below the knee, and find prayer position with your hands. While pushing down firmly on the standing leg as if pressing the floor away, find strength in your belly, press your palms firmly together and breathe very slowly. Laugh if you fall out of the pose. Try standing near a wall, if you need more support (Figure 8.11).

Twists (e.g. Figure 8.12) are great for digestion. Be sure to keep your hips facing forward, your collarbone open, and twist from the belly. Inhale to get length, exhale to twist further. Inversions cause the blood flow to move to the head and brain and away from the feet and legs. Both calming and exhilarating, an inversion can be as simple as putting your legs up a wall.

An Energizing Flow Sequence

Are you ready to flow from one pose to the next? Try the following sun salutation sequence:

- Stand tall with your feet about inner hip width apart. Place your palms together in prayer position in front of your heart. On a big inhale and with great joy, spread your arms out wide and then lift them towards the sky (Figure 8.13). Make sure your shoulder blades remain firmly anchored in your back and as far away from your ears as possible. Imagine that you're greeting the sun and drawing in its warmth and energy. As you slowly exhale, spread your arms out to the sides like giant wings and with a flat back and your navel pulled in, dive forward, bending from your hips. Allow your hands to touch the floor in front of you by bending your knees. Let your head just hang.

Figure 8.10 Tree pose

Figure 8.11 Supported Tree pose

Figure 8.12 Seated twist

- Now extend your right leg straight back behind you as you take another big inhalation, coming into a lunge position (Figure 8.14). Feel the power in your right leg. Feel the power in your right heel as it pushes back, as if to touch a wall behind you. Take a few slow breaths and then place your left leg beside your right leg and come down to Child's pose. Alternatively, if you want something more energizing, lift your buttocks up, and let your head hang gently between your shoulders, coming into Downward Facing Dog (Figure 8.15).

- A good pose for quieting an overactive mind, Downward Facing Dog can be a resting pose between more challenging movements. Both an inversion and a backbend, in Downward Facing Dog you continue to take strong breaths and maintain awareness of good alignment.

- From either Child's pose or Downward Facing Dog, inhale into a lunge by moving your right leg forward until it rests on the floor between your hands (Figure 8.16). Exhale as you walk your back leg in to return to a forward fold. Place your hand on your hips and as you inhale, slowly roll up to a standing position.

Expect to find many variations of sun salutations. Most include a gentle backbend, either Cobra or Upward Facing Dog, as part of the sequence. One of most enjoyable aspects of saluting the sun can be the sense of flowing from one posture to the next. You're literally moving on the power of the breath. As breath links with movement, the process resembles a dance.

Restorative Poses

What if you're ready for complete surrender? The following restorative poses are good ones to enjoy before going to bed.

LEGS UP THE WALL

The gentlest inversion, this pose refreshes the legs and promotes a restful sleep (Figure 8.17). To begin, sit sidesaddle so that your right side is near the wall. As you turn to face the wall, swing your legs up the wall. Get your buttocks as close as possible to the wall. If you're too far away, lift up onto your elbows and shimmy closer. Let your arms rest by your sides with your palms open. Try placing a blanket under your lower back and a rolled up towel under your neck. Close your eyes and feel your breath as you melt into the ground beneath you.

Figure 8.13 Upward Facing Mountain pose

Figure 8.14 Lunge with right leg back

Figure 8.15 Downward Facing Dog

Figure 8.16 Lunge with left leg back

Stay in the pose for as long as you like. When you're ready to come out, bend your knees toward your chest. Roll onto your right side and rest there for several breath cycles.

Figure 8.17 Legs up the wall

RECLINING BUTTERFLY POSE

Lying on the floor or a mat, place a folded blanket, a bolster, or a firm cushion under your back, just beneath your shoulder blades (Figure 8.18). Bring the soles of your feet to touch. Arrange a cushion or bolster under your knees or one smaller pillow under each knee. If desired, place a rolled-up towel under your neck to allow the back of your head to rest comfortably. Let your arms roll out to your sides, palms facing up. Close your eyes, sink into the supports, breathe slowly, and enjoy the wonderful sensation of complete surrender.

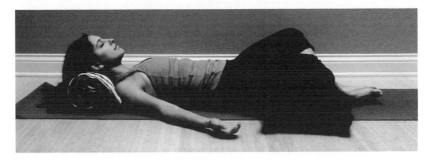

Figure 8.18 Reclining Butterfly pose

Yoga for Kids

Children of all ages love yoga. You can find programs tailor-made for preschoolers, as well as practices that would appeal to adolescents. In addition to promoting a calming effect, yoga builds strength, balance, attention, and coordination, making it ideal for children with autism, ADHD, and other handicapping conditions. All of the benefits enumerated for adults apply to children as well, but the primary reason that yoga is great for kids: it's fun! If you work with children or are a parent or caregiver, try practicing together. To help you get started, I've listed a number of good books and DVDs in Appendix 1.

Troubleshooting: What Could Go Wrong with Yoga?

If you prescribe yoga and the experience turns out to be unpleasant or anxiety-provoking, find out exactly what went wrong. Was the class was too advanced, too easy, too crowded, or too warm? Did the teacher give unclear directions or fail to provide enough individualized attention? Did your client attempt to practice from a book or DVD as a first experience and need more guidance? Did you suggest a few poses and receive negative feedback?

First and foremost, recommend a well-trained teacher. Beginning with a few private sessions to learn basic principles of alignment should be considered if financially feasible. Classes should offer options to accommodate all levels. For example, the use of blocks can make up for lack of mobility and prevent injury. If a particular class or style of yoga isn't working, find another one that may be more suitable. If you recommend a particular pose or series of poses, make sure that you're aware of any physical limitations beforehand.

Stay within your comfort zone, only suggesting poses that you've personally tried and enjoyed. If you receive negative feedback, let it be and move on to something else in your toolkit, recommend joining a class, or prescribe a different style of yoga.

What If Yoga Really isn't My Cup of Tea?

I chose to write about the benefits of yoga, but two other time-honored movement traditions yield similar results: tai chi and qi gong. Consider them as wonderful alternatives if someone has a negative reaction to yoga. They're both described as moving meditations and are extremely gentle to the body.

Taiji, an ancient form of movement that unites mind and body, is believed to restore the flow of *qi*, or energy, and create a state of balance. Qi gong, pronounced "chee-gong," dates back at least two thousand years. Similar to taiji, by integrating meditation, breathing, and movement, the practice helps to resolve energy blockages, so that *qi* can flow freely.

Putting It All Together: Living the Yoga Way

Practice yoga to maintain a calm state and prevent the onset of panic by weaving yoga poses into daily life. But how does anyone find time to fit yoga into a busy schedule? While attending a class offers the most benefits, any amount of time yields positive results. Set an intention to practice for 20 minutes every morning and evening. If that's not working, commit to 10 minutes. Look for opportunities to strike a yoga pose whenever the spirit moves you.

Begin each morning with three to five energizing sun salutations. Take advantage of waiting in line to stand tall in Mountain pose. While attending professional conferences that require sitting for long periods of time, I sit in a cross-legged lotus position and frequently walk to the back of the room to get a shot of energy from a backbend or two.

Try some restorative, anxiety-reducing forward bends while seated in a chair. Place a pillow on your desk or a table in front of you. Sitting comfortably in the chair, put your arms on top of the pillow. Bend forward from the hips, and rest your head on the pillow. Try to keep your back straight. Breathe from your belly very slowly and take ten deep breaths.

You don't need a mat to practice yoga. I like to move into forward bends and twists while on an airplane. Place your right hand behind you on the seat or armrest and your left hand on the outside of your right thigh. Inhale as you slowly turn your torso to the right as far as you can without straining. Let your head be the last to turn. Twist from the belly. Then repeat to the other side. Elongate your spine as you inhale and twist as you exhale.

Yoga can be thought of as a moving meditation that softens the heart. If symptoms of panic escalate, meaningful engagement in a yoga practice can distract from the negative sensations. What a great opportunity awaits you to increase awareness of slow, rhythmical breathing while holding a position or moving from pose to pose! Simultaneously, incorporate wonderful imagery, which can easily be evoked just from the names of the various poses. Feel from the heart as you place your hands in prayer position, let go of irrational thoughts and self-judgment, feel the power of movement, find physical strength, and laugh if you fall down.

Don't forget to emphasize the *practice* in a yoga practice. Practicing regularly and consistently enhances a sense of self-control because you're actively involved in healing and can feel a sense of accomplishment at what your body just mastered.

The spirit of yoga is the spirit of self-acceptance in the present moment. Extend the lessons from the mat to daily living by weaving yoga philosophy into your way of being. Even if you're not actively practicing, commit to an inner practice throughout the day to shed anxiety and become more at ease. Upon awakening, set your intention. Maybe you visualize a calm, panic-free day.

A yoga practice can be the one consistent thing that you can rely on wherever you go. When you need your practice, it will be there. It doesn't require a mat, a block, or a cushion, or fancy yoga attire. It's a state of mind. Through this practice, you can deal with the battles in your mind and find the inner balance that will bring peace to your life.

CHAPTER 9

Nourish Yourself

Eating Real Foods, Adding the Right Supplements, and Removing Toxins

"Let food be thy medicine."
—*Hippocrates ca 400 BC*

In previous chapters, we looked at the benefits of replacing negative thoughts, images, and breathing patterns with more soothing ones and adding physical movement and positive connections to quiet the mind and body. Now it's time to dig deeper and look for causes of panic that are frequently overlooked. What irritating foods may be contributing to panic and anxiety? What toxic chemicals assault the body? What nutrients may be lacking? Is supplementation with vitamins, minerals, or herbs helpful?

By venturing into nutrition, you may be stepping beyond your comfort zone. Most mental health professionals, myself included, had no training in this area. We were educated to treat the mind, not the body. I always ask new clients to keep a three-day log of everything they eat and drink, but it's rare to see questions about diet or chemical exposure on standard psychological intake forms.

Food is not just calories. The right amount of the right foods can be more powerful than any medicine, while the wrong amount of the wrong foods leads to harmful consequences. There's a significant connection between what we put into our bodies and panic. But I did not realize that back in 1980.

I was in Palo Alto, California at the time for a workshop on Type A behavior and heart disease. Although unaccustomed to traveling without my husband, I successfully navigated renting a car and driving from San Francisco to Palo Alto. Free from fears, excited about the conference, and looking forward to exploring the new surroundings, I decided to take a walk through a beautiful shopping center close to my hotel. Coming upon a shop filled with chocolate truffles, I chose to indulge. Why not? What's the harm in sampling some and bringing a treat back to my hotel room?

At the time, and for many years prior, I was seriously addicted to sugar in all forms. A major portion of my diet consisted of cookies, candy bars, ice cream, and cakes. On a "good day," I thought I made better choices by eating cereal, bagels, or some pasta. Vegetables? Maybe some carrots on a "diet day." Protein? That only crossed my mind when I wanted to lose weight fast to fit into a dress for a weekend party.

Returning to my hotel room with a bag of chocolate truffles, I bit into one, but before I knew it I had finished all three of them. But so what? I was on vacation. About two hours later as I was about to get into bed, I noticed my heart was racing. You can probably guess what happened next: chest pains, difficulty breathing, light-headedness; in other words, full-blown panic. I remember thinking how ironic it was that I was having a heart attack while attending a conference where all we did was discuss heart disease. I even called down to the front desk to say I was "really sick" and needed medical attention. Luckily, they were inefficient because I turned on the television, became distracted, started to feel a little better and eventually fell asleep.

Analyzing the above scenario, the precipitating factors could have been being alone in an unfamiliar setting and the stirring up of old fears about heart disease due to the conference theme. But those risk factors weren't enough to "send me over the edge." In fact, I remember feeling relaxed and happy. The event that triggered the panic episode was the overconsumption of sugar and caffeine. Looking back, I'm certain I would have had a peaceful night if only I had eliminated the "bad stuff" and nourished myself with the "good stuff."

Remove the Bad Stuff

A key principle of functional medicine involves taking out what's bad for you. That's easier said than done, as we may not be aware of just what's in the food we're eating or the products we're using, and the effects they're having on brain health.

There's considerable research to support the relationship between food and mood, but when we think of anxiety, we typically don't associate it with nutritional needs. Yet poor food choices and eating habits can create constant stress. Some foods promote a calm, quiet state, while others promote anxiety. We're only just beginning to explore the effect of environmental toxins on brain health. The following discussion only scratches the surface of these fascinating topics. For more information, refer to the resources listed in Appendix 1.

Eliminate Irritating Foods and Drinks

The sugar-laden fast foods we consume are overly refined and processed, and filled with chemicals and hormones. These "food-like" substances, so far removed from the fresh foods that our great-grandparents ate, tax our gastrointestinal tract and detoxification systems, signal the overproduction of insulin, and stress the adrenal glands.

SUGAR

Why is sugar so addictive? Along with alcohol, heroin, morphine, and other opiates, sugar stimulates the release of endorphins, the "feel-good" neurotransmitters that help create a sense of wellbeing, at least for a short period of time. We may crave sugar when endorphin levels are low in an attempt to rebalance our brain chemistry. But hitting the body with this sudden influx of endorphins causes it to be metabolized too quickly. The momentary endorphin "high" is followed by a longer-lasting "low," which sets off a physical craving for more sugar. As a result, the more often you consume sweets, the more intensely you crave them.

Sugar places an enormous stress on the body, not only triggering a surge in the stress hormones cortisol and adrenaline, but also leading to inflammation due to the overproduction of insulin. After eating something sweet, blood sugar levels may shoot up too quickly, resulting in a corresponding rush of insulin production. When insulin levels rise, blood sugar levels drop too low, resulting in wide swings in blood sugar and, ultimately, overall low blood sugar, referred to as hypoglycemia. Dizziness, disorientation, mental fog, fatigue, trembling, heart palpitations, weakness, or irritability have been associated with low blood sugar levels. Blood sugar disregulation may result in feeling "high" 20–30 minutes after consuming sugar.

If blood sugar levels are too high, such as immediately after eating a big piece of cake, you might feel revved up, agitated or overly stimulated. I'm all too familiar with this syndrome and in hindsight, recognize it as a major contributor to my panic attacks. Sometimes people who awaken in a state of panic do so because blood sugar levels are generally lowest in the early morning due to having fasted all night.

Our bodies need carbohydrates for fuel, but not all carbohydrates affect blood sugar and insulin production in the same way. I just finished a dinner of brown rice and beans. These carbohydrates have lots of fiber, a tough substance which takes a long time to be broken down by the digestive enzymes and converted into glucose for fuel. Consequently, you won't experience a sugar rush. By providing a slow, steady release of glucose into the system, including the brain, carbohydrates in the form of whole grains and beans offer a stable way to feel alert, balanced, and energized.

Processed foods containing sugar or flour, such as cookies, crackers, breads, and most cereals are already broken down, which means the body doesn't have to work very hard to convert them to blood sugar. As a result, they send blood sugar levels skyrocketing, followed by the inevitable crash that leaves us craving another fix to raise our blood sugar. The sudden influx of glucose triggers an equally sudden surge of insulin. Concentrated fruit juices and soft drinks may be the worst offenders, as they jolt the system with a "shot of sugar."

Overconsumption of sugar, amongst other factors, may lead to an overgrowth of the yeast variety *Candida albicans*. Symptoms associated with this condition, including feelings of unreality, "brain fog," and chest tightness, mimic panic sensations. It should be pointed out that many in the medical community are skeptical regarding the validity of this condition. However, anyone with sugar cravings who describes these symptoms may be suffering from *Candida* overgrowth.

CAFFEINE

When you consume caffeine, the sympathetic branch of the autonomic nervous system turns on and releases adrenaline. Norepinephrine levels elevate, and as a result you feel wide-awake. This may be okay for some, but individuals prone to panic may overreact to substances which affect the central nervous system. Drinking even one cup of coffee may trigger a panic attack. What's more, that cup of coffee you drank in the morning to wake up may stay in your system for longer than you realize and can contribute to feeling anxious throughout the day and even into the evening. As an alternative, consider switching to green tea. Although high in caffeine, it also contains l-theanine, a nutrient that blocks the absorption of caffeine. I drink green tea all day long and invite clients to share a cup with me.

Look for Hidden Food Allergies and Intolerances

Allergies are easy to detect: you eat something and immediately develop a rash or hives. Some allergic reactions may not be as obvious, such as heart palpitations, dizziness, or other sensations associated with panic. Food sensitivities or intolerances may be even less apparent. Although food sensitivities may be pervasive in modern societies, we could be intolerant of certain foods and not know it. We're often sensitive to the foods we crave the most, and these cravings may have led to a state of imbalance. Gluten (a protein found primarily in wheat, barley, and rye), dairy, corn, and soy are common offenders. Our immune cells react to these foods as foreign invaders and activate the stress response, leading to inflammation.

How do you know if you have hidden food sensitivities? Although blood tests are available that measure the number of antibodies produced in reaction to a wide range of foods, the most accurate and most economical way to find out which foods you may be sensitive to involves going on an elimination diet. One option would be to refrain from eating gluten, dairy, and sugar for six weeks, as these are the most problematic foods for optimal brain health. During this time, also refrain from eating processed foods with chemicals and additives, such as artificial sweeteners, monosodium glutamate (MSG), and nitrates.

Children with autism, attention deficit disorder, and learning disabilities may be particularly at risk for food intolerances. Dr. Martha Herbert, a professor of neurology at Harvard Medical School who specializes in autism research, published an article in *Clinical Neuropsychiatry,* "Autism: A brain disorder, or a disorder that affects the brain?", in which she proposed that behavior patterns found in children with autism may be rooted in digestive and immune system abnormalities (Herbert 2005). Her work looks at the influence of diet and environmental toxins.

Eliminate Chemical Toxins

Consider for a moment the sheer volume of chemicals that we're exposed to on a daily basis. We eat food laden with additives, artificial colors, artificial flavours, and pesticides. We're exposed to toxic environmental pollutants in our homes, our workplaces, and when we step outside. Personal care products and toiletries, such as shampoos, deodorants, lotions, moisturizers, aftershave, cosmetics, perfumes, and hand sanitizers all contain chemicals and dyes. Add household-cleaning products, insecticides, plastics, and the heavy metals lurking in sources ranging from food to dental work. Now throw into the mix the increasing number of electronic devices such as microwave ovens, wireless routers, cordless telephones and cellular phones that create electromagnetic fields.

These hundreds of chemical substances are potentially toxic to the brain and can provoke reactions that we may not be aware of. Chemical exposure adds to the overall stress level by overtaxing the adrenal glands, and may either directly or indirectly contribute to a panic reaction. Symptoms associated with sensitivity to chemicals include "brain fog," irritability, and insomnia. I've personally seen a number of children diagnosed with panic disorder who were referred to me for psychotherapy. Many of them had also been diagnosed with sensory-integration problems. My hunch was that they were reacting to environmental chemicals, as they often complained about sensitivity to clothing fibers or certain odors. Panic symptoms lessened when exposure levels decreased.

My intake evaluation, whether with adults or children, includes questions about possible environmental stressors. It's wise to eliminate as many toxins as possible from food, cleaning products, and personal care items. The Environmental Working Group is a wonderful resource where more information can be obtained about this topic (see Appendix 1: Resources).

Repair the Body

Heal the Gut

We have a second brain: it's called the gut. This brain possesses its own nervous system, the enteric nervous system, which contains more neurons than the spinal cord. The majority of serotonin is produced by these nerve cells and most of the fibers in the vagus nerve carry information from the gut to the brain. The brain experiences everything that happens in the gut either directly via the central nervous system, or indirectly due to immune activity. When you get "butterflies" in your stomach or have a strong "gut reaction," that's the gut–brain connection at work.

One of the Institute for Functional Medicine's mantras, "Heal the gut," implies that in order for the brain to be in balance, the gut must be in balance. Gastrointestinal (GI) conditions, such as irritable bowel syndrome, have been linked with anxiety, based on the assumption that an anxious mind leads to GI disturbances. Now there's evidence that anxiety may originate in the gut.

The beneficial bacteria residing in the gut perform many critical functions, including influencing brain chemistry. In a study that appeared in the journal *Gastroenterology*, researchers showed that when the normal bacterial content of the gut was disrupted due to antibiotic use, an increase in brain-derived neurotrophic factor (BDNF) occurred (Bercik *et al.* 2010). BDNF has been linked to anxiety as well as depression. More research is needed on the benefit of supplementation with probiotics (various strains of friendly bacteria) for the treatment of anxiety and mood disorders, particularly those associated with gastrointestinal conditions.

Put Out the Fire of Inflammation

Eating a "junk food" diet of highly processed foods, the presence of food allergens or intolerances, and environmental stressors all contribute to an inflammatory response within the body. The brain may not be insulated from inflammation. Anxiety, depression, or a host of other conditions previously thought to be "all in the mind" might be the end result of having a brain that's "on fire."

Balance Your Hormones

Maybe you're experiencing heart palpitations, dizziness, or dry mouth, all familiar signs of panic disorder. But how many of the following symptoms also sound familiar?

- Tired upon waking.

- Difficulty falling asleep and/or staying asleep.

- Feeling both wired and exhausted.

- Falling asleep in the afternoon or dozing while reading.

- Generalized weakness.

- Weight gain around the midline.

- Loss of muscle mass.

- Frequent headaches.

- Swollen ankles.

- Hypoglycemia.

- Needing caffeine or sugary snacks to get through the day.

- Irritability.

- Listlessness.

- Low sex drive.

- Trouble concentrating.

We tend to think of someone with panic disorder as "wired." But it's possible to be both "tired and wired" at the same time due to adrenal exhaustion, which develops when the glands cannot adequately meet the demands of chronic stress.

Excessive production of cortisol leads to imbalances in the production of other hormones, including insulin, thyroid, and sex-hormones, and contributes to digestive problems, depression, difficulty concentrating, memory problems, and, last but not least, anxiety. Eventually, adrenal fatigue sets in as the output of cortisol diminishes due to overstimulation. To learn more about adrenal functioning and how to restore balance, refer to *Are You Tired and Wired?* by Marcelle Pick (2011).

Boost Energy Metabolism and Enhance Detoxification

Panic attacks might be a signal that something is out of balance. While the traditional route just looks at bringing the mind into a calm, balanced state, functional medicine addresses the bigger picture. Besides paying attention to the role of the gut, the presence of inflammation and hormonal imbalances, two other key components for health are assessed: energy metabolism at a cellular level and detoxification pathways. The latter involves the proper elimination of metabolic waste products and environmental toxins. For an in-depth discussion of these areas, I suggest reading the chapters on energy metabolism and detoxification in the *Textbook of Functional Medicine* (Jones 2010).

To create balance in the mind, these core processes must function well. How do we create this optimal state? Think food first. We restore the body by feeding it the raw materials essential for life: whole, real foods rich in nutrients in combination with the other ingredients we've covered so far, such as relaxed breathing, good thoughts, exercise that's fun, and social connections.

Add the Good Stuff: Staying Nutritionally Balanced

A well-fed brain equals a healthy brain. Building brain cells and keeping the communications systems running efficiently requires the raw materials that come from food. There's even a field of study called nutrigenomics that addresses how food affects genes. Various foods contain information that either turn on the expression of particular genes or turn it off. Yet most of us know very little about nutrition.

Everything we eat affects stress levels and emotional states. Both the macronutrients (proteins, fats, and carbohydrates) and micronutrients (vitamins, minerals, and phytonutrients, the colorful pigments in plant foods) act as powerful neurochemicals. A deficiency in even one of these nutrients creates imbalance and compromises brain health. As a result, our response to stress deteriorates and we react with anxiety or depression. Furthermore, if we're trying to cope with chronic stress, the need for a balanced blend of nutrients increases. Don't let this discussion about macro- and micronutrients scare you. I'm not going to turn this chapter into a nutrition textbook. For that, refer to *Clinical Nutrition, A Functional Approach* (Liska *et al.* 2004).

Feeding your mind the right nutrients means eating real food. I love a small guidebook by Michael Pollan called *Food Rules* and often recommend it to clients. Pollan advises readers to "eat food, not too much and mostly plants." He suggests avoiding anything your great-grandmother wouldn't recognize as food (Pollan 2009).

In *Macrobiotics for Life*, macrobiotic expert Simon Brown discusses the idea that foods contain a life force or living energy, which can have an almost immediate effect on energy level and mood (Brown 2009). It's possible to become more aware of the changes that may occur after consuming particular foods. Try this experiment: begin by breathing to reach a calm state and then eat something, such as a handful of raw nuts. Notice everything you feel after eating. Then repeat this exercise with another food, such as a banana or an apple. Try eating a cooked food. Notice any differences in mental clarity or energy level. Some foods may have a cooling effect, while others induce a warming response. Consume mostly raw vegetables, fruits, and salads one day, and then eat cooked stews, thick soups, or casseroles the following day. Raw foods might make you feel lighter and more energized, while cooked foods lead to feeling satisfied, content, and warm.

You don't need a degree in nutrition to advise clients to pay attention to everything they eat and notice how particular foods make them feel. You do, however, need to "walk the walk and talk the talk" by paying attention to your own food choices. Does eating a sugar-laden, over-processed snack food result in you feeling calm and contented? Observe how removing the bad stuff and adding nourishing foods leads to increased resiliency and less anxiety. Inform clients that the most important decision they make each day is what they choose to place on the end of their forks, words of advice I learned from Dr. Mark Hyman.

A Healthy Diet

Just what constitutes a healthy food? Look to fresh vegetables, fruits, healthy fats, beans, whole grains, and good-quality animal sources of proteins such as tiny fish (which are lower in mercury than larger fish), eggs, poultry, and grass-fed beef. Whenever possible, choose organic vegetables (to reduce the toxic effects of pesticides) and antibiotic- and hormone-free eggs and poultry. The top three anti-anxiety "medicines" to add to your diet and recommend to clients are dark green vegetables, protein (particularly at breakfast), and healthy fats.

VEGETABLES

It seems our mothers were right after all when they admonished us to eat our vegetables. A plant-based diet (vegetables first, then fruits, particularly berries) boosts the production of glutathione, an antioxidant critical for brain health and energy production, which also protects against oxidation, controls inflammation, and helps with elimination of toxins. Specific nutrients in plants, called phytonutrients, activate the Nrf2 pathway, which in turn generates glutathione production at the cellular level. We can protect our brain and enhance its functioning by eating a variety of vegetables, including kale, collard greens, Swiss chard, bok choy, parsley, cabbage, arugula, radishes, broccoli, and mustard greens.

If I want to feel calmer, I eat more vegetables. Due to their light, watery quality, vegetables help energy move freely throughout the body, resulting in a peaceful feeling. However, frying, grilling, roasting, or baking these foods may not have the same beneficial effects as eating them raw, steamed, stewed, lightly boiled, fermented, or in a soup.

GOOD-QUALITY PROTEINS

Without an adequate amount of protein at each meal, the brain can't function properly. Proteins contain amino acids, the raw materials needed to make neurotransmitters. Without a steady supply of amino acids, the body has no way to manufacture neurotransmitters.

If you're eating a breakfast loaded with sugar and refined flours, such as a bowl of dry cereal or a sweet roll, switch to a protein-based breakfast and notice how different you feel. Do you have more energy and increased alertness? Are you calmer? If you start the day with eggs or a smoothie containing a protein powder (see the Appendix 2 for a simple recipe), you'll be getting all the amino acids needed to produce the neurotransmitters that are essential for optimal brain functioning. If you eat a small protein snack mid-morning and afternoon, you'll also be feeding your mind some wellness.

HEALTHY FATS

Do you need an oil change? The brain is mostly fat, and omega-3 fatty acids, comprising docosaheyaenic acid (DHA) and eicosapentaenic acid (EPA), are the most important ingredients for brain health. Not only a critical building block for the membranes that surround brain cells, DHA also plays a role in the transmission of information from one neuron to the next, controls inflammation, and modulates gene expression for the production of BDNF. EPA also controls inflammation, and low levels have been associated with depression.

Unfortunately, we're eating more refined, omega-6 oils, including corn, soy, and safflower oils, and fewer omega-3 fats, which come primarily from wild-caught fish. As our diets have become more processed, the ratio of omega-6 to omega-3 fats has increased from the ideal of 1:1 to as high as 20:1.

To increase intake of omega-3 fatty acids, eat sardines, anchovies, wild salmon, and halibut. The other category of healthy oils, the monounsaturated omega-9s, are powerful anti-inflammatory agents. Consider using olive oil and avocados as your main sources of fat.

WHOLE GRAINS AND LEGUMES

What constitutes a whole grain? It's not a grain that's been milled into flour to make breads or pastas. Although many people believe a whole grain equals wholewheat bread or pasta, a whole grain is the actual kernel, such as brown rice or quinoa (an ancient grain that's a complete protein). These foods may boost serotonin levels.

In addition to being a good source of protein and fiber, legumes, such as beans, peas, and lentils, contain B vitamins, magnesium, potassium, and zinc. These nutrients play a key role in stress reduction. Sit down to a meal of beans, brown rice, and sautéed dark, leafy greens, and you've just served yourself a powerful anti-anxiety medication.

FERMENTED FOODS

Fermented or cultured foods, such as yogurt, sauerkraut, kimchi (spicy fermented cabbage popular in Korea), and miso (fermented soybean paste) contain probiotic bacteria. These microorganisms play a key role in digestion. While scientific evidence attests to the gastrointestinal benefits, including reducing the symptoms of diarrhea and irritable bowel syndrome, new research is exploring the effect of probiotics on brain functioning. These beneficial bacteria may affect GABA, the inhibitory neurotransmitter that reduces the activity of neurons. In an animal study conducted by Dr. Javier Bravo and Professor John Cryan at University College Cork in Ireland, rats fed foods containing probiotics exhibited less anxiety and released less stress hormone.

WATER

Dizziness, disorientation, and feelings of faintness are symptoms of panic, but they can also be signs of dehydration. A rule of thumb: drink half your body weight in ounces each day. Advise clients to sip water throughout the day and always have a water bottle handy. If panic develops, respiration rate increases, sweating may develop, or they feel hot and clammy. Drinking water can effectively put a stop to these sensations. The experience can be enriched if the process becomes a mindful meditation (e.g. noticing all the details involved in taking those sips of water).

Old Habits Die Hard

What to do if someone just won't eat their vegetables or healthy fats and has difficulty getting enough protein because they prefer a carbohydrate-heavy diet? A green smoothie may be the answer for both adults and children who fall into this category. The drink can provide a perfect blend of protein, fats, and carbohydrates in the form of fruits and vegetables. But more importantly, it tastes yummy, and can solve the "what do I eat for breakfast?" problem. Green smoothies can even be poured into ice cube trays and converted into a frozen treat so that kids of all ages can "lick their vegetables." I've included my favorite green smoothie recipe in Appendix 2.

Soups can be another good option, especially in colder climates where smoothies may sound unappealing in the dead of winter. When my daughters were little, I disguised all types of vegetables, legumes, and healthy fats in pureed soups.

Raw nuts and seeds make great snacks. Experiment with all varieties, including almonds, walnuts, pecans, cashews, hazelnuts, and Brazil nuts (high in selenium). Rather than sticking with peanut butter, try other nut butters, such as almond butter or cashew butter. My mid-morning snack today consisted of an apple with some almond butter. Also incorporate seeds into your diet, including pumpkin seeds, sesame seeds, sunflower seeds, and hemp seeds. These can be ground into delicious, creamy butters and are a good option if someone is allergic to tree nuts.

Any positive dietary change represents a step in the right direction. Maybe that means adding some lettuce and tomato to a sandwich or tossing some kale or parsley into a prepared or canned soup. Just contemplating adding more whole, unprocessed foods and eliminating the bad stuff is a great beginning on the journey towards considering food as medicine.

How, When, Where, How Much, and Why We Eat Matters

We can design the perfect, most nutritionally balanced meal, but if we're gulping it down in a hurry, not taking the time to chew it properly, reading or answering emails at the same time, overeating, or eating for reasons other than hunger, then we're stressing our system.

Eating quickly and not taking the time to properly chew and taste our food leads to incomplete digestion, which can be a significant source of chronic stress. Digestion begins in the mouth, where predigestion must occur to prevent partially digested food from passing through the intestines and fermenting, causing gas, bloating, and inadequate absorption of nutrients. As a rule of thumb, chew your food 40 times before swallowing it.

How meals are timed throughout the day matters. Are you running out of the house without breakfast, skipping lunch or coming home famished and eating a large meal late at night? If so, your adrenal glands aren't happy. The body, brain included, constantly needs energy from blood sugar, even while asleep. By going for extended periods of time without eating and getting too hungry, blood sugar levels drop, which creates stress and taxes the adrenal glands.

To maintain a balanced state throughout the day, follow these guidelines: eat breakfast; eat every two to three hours to balance blood sugar and insulin levels; eat your biggest meal early in the day, make dinner the lightest meal; stop eating two to three hours before bedtime.

Just as important to consider as what, how and when you're eating is why you're eating, which may be the most difficult pattern to change. When anxious, many people turn to food, and they don't turn to broccoli or kale. Instead, they reach for a comfort food, usually some combination of sugar, salt, and fat. Are you using snack foods or sweets as a major form of stress reduction? Are you eating without awareness and subsequently eating so much that you feel stuffed and bloated?

Once upon a time eating was referred to as "dining." Why not make eating a calming, relaxing experience? Use all of the tools we've focused on to dine with mindfulness. Begin by breathing slowly and with your belly as you approach a meal and imagine the blend of life-sustaining nutrients you'll be taking in. Warm your heart with gratitude for the food that's in front of you. Abandon any irrational ideas, such as "I need dessert." Distract yourself from disturbing thoughts and sensations by maintaining awareness of the food you're eating, including the array of colors, aromas, textures, shapes, and tastes on your plate. Apply moment-by-moment awareness to chewing and swallowing. As you continue to belly breathe, observe how your stomach feels. Notice when you're beginning to feel full.

Approaching meals in a calm manner, eating mindfully, and refraining from combining meals with other activities leads to parasympathetic dominance. Remember that proper digestion takes place when the sympathetic alarm system shuts off and the relaxation response takes over. Likewise, the more efficient the digestive process, the calmer and more balanced we feel.

When Food isn't Enough: The Use of Supplements

A dietary supplement is just that, something to be added to a healthy, balanced diet. Working with supplements can resemble stepping onto a minefield. There are thousands of products to choose from, and sometimes conflicting information and recommendations emerging from the latest research studies. Healthcare professionals feel confused and overwhelmed, so expect clients to experience these feelings as well. Some may already be sold on supplements and eagerly purchase whatever they see advertised. Others are adamantly against supplementing their diets, either out of fear or because someone, often a physician, has warned them that supplements can't help them or could even be dangerous.

I follow a simple rule: food first, then cautiously recommend good-quality supplements to make up for any deficiencies that can't be overcome with dietary changes. Remember that finding balance remains the primary goal. Often supplements are necessary because our diets are out of balance. For example, if someone hates the taste of fish or eats primarily processed foods full of omega-6 oils, then supplementing with fish oils makes sense. Likewise, even if someone eats a ton of dark green vegetables every day, they might still be deficient in magnesium because the soil in which the greens were grown may lack this important mineral.

Finding balance implies guarding against reductionistic thinking. I've been emphasizing an integrative approach throughout the book and therefore hesitate to break down the various nutrients because it's easy to fall into the trap of viewing them in isolation. Just as having only one tool won't help clients stop a panic attack, recommending a specific supplement because you heard somewhere that it may reduce anxiety may not be helpful and, in some cases, can even be harmful.

Merely substituting a supplement for a prescription medication isn't functional medicine. Similarly, even if a particular supplement may be beneficial, taking more of it isn't necessarily better. There's an old saying, "the remedy is in the dose." Think of an inverted U-shaped curve: none isn't good and too much is just as bad. Also keep in mind that deficiencies may be due to inadequate breakdown and absorption. Another consideration involves the form of a particular supplement, for example synthetic compared to natural, or tablet versus sublingual or liquid. Some inexpensive brands add fillers, binders, sweeteners, and even artificial preservatives and coloring.

Follow dosage recommendations carefully and be aware of any drug–nutrient interaction effects, the specific time of day that's best to take particular supplements, which supplements should be taken together and which should never be combined, and whether or not they should be taken on an empty stomach or with food. Given all of these considerations, it's important to stay abreast of the current research literature, gain experience by attending continuing education courses, and either consult with or refer clients to a healthcare professional who has training in the use of nutritional supplements and herbal medicine.

The following discussion provides an overview of the most important nutraceuticals that are hard to obtain from foods alone. They have the best safety records, but if in doubt, seek consultation or refer clients to a qualified nutritionist. As you go through this list, consider your own nutritional needs.

FISH OILS

Are you eating wild salmon, mackerel, or sardines at least several times a week? Probably not, so it's wise to supplement with fish oil to obtain a sufficient amount of omega-3 fatty acids, the brain food discussed earlier.

As with other recommendations, if you choose to prescribe fish oils, be specific. Rather than suggesting that someone go out and get some fish oils, write down a specific brand. Make sure the product is molecularly distilled, as contaminants such as heavy metals have been found in discounted brands. Many companies offer fish oils for children that are flavored. Some even look like fish or gummy worms. Although there's no set rule regarding dosages, adults usually begin with 1000 mg per day and work up to 2000 mg, although higher amounts can be suggested for short-term use (typically up to 4000 mg. per day in divided doses). For children, begin with 500 mg and work up to 1000 mg.

B-COMPLEX VITAMINS

Think of B vitamins as the "anti-stress vitamins." They help the brain transform amino acids into neurotransmitters such as serotonin, norepinephrine, and dopamine and can help keep cortisol levels within a normal range throughout the day. Vitamins B1, B2 (riboflavin), B3 (niacin), and B9 (folate) play a role in the process of abstract thinking. A deficiency in vitamin B6 has been linked to hyperventilation and panic. Stress depletes your store of these nutrients. Also keep in mind that certain medications, such as acid blockers, also referred to as proton pump inhibitors, and antidepressants, deplete B12, essential for energy production. Occasionally, supplementation with a B-complex may provoke an anxiety reaction, most likely due to a genetic variant. Therefore, begin with a low dose and work up slowly. Choose quality brands that don't use synthetic forms of these nutrients.

VITAMIN C

Vitamin C, generally regarded as a potent antioxidant that stimulates the immune system and promotes wound healing, also wards off some of the detrimental effects of stress by lowering cortisol levels. Even a slight deficiency may result in an elevation of cortisol.

MAGNESIUM

Looking for a stress antidote? Start with magnesium, one of the most powerful relaxation and anti-anxiety agents. Magnesium ensures the proper functioning of the nervous system, as well as the conversion of carbohydrates, proteins, and fats into energy.

Although needs increase during times of increased stress, deficiencies in this mineral may be reaching epidemic proportions, as the typical highly processed diet contains practically no magnesium. Sources of magnesium include dark-green vegetables, sea vegetables, nuts, and beans, but our soil has become depleted over the years. Chronic stress and consumption of alcohol, salt, coffee, sugar, and phosphoric acid (found in soft drinks) decreases magnesium. Even more is lost through excessive sweating, diuretics, and the use of antibiotics or proton pump inhibitors.

Given the challenges of getting enough magnesium from foods alone, supplementing should be considered. Magnesium glycinate and magnesium citrate are safe and highly absorbable forms. Liquid magnesium is also available, which can be a good option for children. I often refer to magnesium as "nature's Valium" and recommend taking some about one hour before bedtime. The dosage range is generally between 250 and 500 mg. Magnesium can also be combined with calcium to promote sleep.

OTHER IMPORTANT VITAMINS AND MINERALS

A chapter on nutrition wouldn't be complete without some mention of vitamin D. Our bodies just can't seem to make enough of this key vitamin because we're not out in the sun for eight hours a day without sunscreen. Related to regulation of the immune system, cell health and mood, vitamin D may indirectly affect anxiety levels. Levels should be checked regularly as part of routine blood work-ups with a 25 (OH) vitamin D test, and although there's some controversy as to what represents an ideal blood level and an appropriate dosage for supplementation, most experts are now recommending 2000 IU (International Units) for adults and 1000 IU for children.

Although I've only highlighted the importance of a few key vitamins and minerals, others to keep in mind are iron, zinc, copper, selenium, potassium and calcium. All are critical for optimum health and the maintenance of a balanced state. At the very least, assess to make sure that clients are taking a good-quality multi-vitamin supplement as insurance against deficits.

The Power of Spices

If food is medicine, then spices are some of the most potent medicines available. Contrary to the popular belief that spices make foods "hot," most spices are aromatic, not fiery. Healers have used them for medicinal purposes for thousands of years. Sanskrit writings from India 3000 years ago and ancient medical texts from China describe the many therapeutic uses of spices. Recently, studies on animal populations have been conducted in India and Asia to validate the effects of specific spices on cortisol levels. Following is a brief listing of the spices associated with lowering anxiety. To learn more about these wonderful agents, refer to *Healing Spices* by Dr. Bharat Aggarwal (2011). Feel free to recommend spices because they smell yummy and enhance the flavor of foods, but keep in mind the importance of balance. A little may be good, but too much can be just as bad as none at all.

BASIL

According to researchers in India, several compounds in basil extract have anti-stress effects and may help to nourish the adrenal glands and normalize cortisol levels.

CORIANDER

One of the world's oldest spices, coriander has traditionally been recommended for relief of anxiety and insomnia. In animal studies it's been shown to act as a sedative and muscle relaxant.

LAVENDER

According to advocates of aromatherapy, the system of healing which uses the aromatic essences of plant oils called essential oils, the scent of lavender is said to be calming and can help promote sleep. Try a drop rubbed into each wrist. (A note of caution: when using essential oils, make sure to get 100 percent pure plant oils, as many products contain a blend of synthetic oils.)

LEMONGRASS

Referred to as "the calming spice," lemongrass is often made into a tea. Native Brazilians drink *abafado* to reduce anxiety. However, a double-blind study in 1986 found it to be no better than a placebo (Leite *et al.* 1986).

MINT

In addition to aiding digestion, peppermint can lower anxiety. Try inhaling mint or using it as a refreshing tea.

NUTMEG

Traditional healers used nutmeg for a variety of conditions, including anxiety. More recently, an animal study in India confirmed its benefits as an anti-anxiety agent (Sonavane *et al.* 2002).

ROSEMARY

According to ancient healers, rosemary has special healing powers. It was often used to treat dizziness. Just breathing rosemary can reduce cortisol levels. Aggarwal (2011) recommends soaking a small piece of cotton with rosemary essential oil, wrapping it in a handkerchief, and sniffing it before and during a test if you suffer from test anxiety.

SAFFRON

Saffron has been used for anxiety and insomnia in traditional medicine. In animal studies crocins, the active components in saffron, were found to have anxiolytic and hypnotic effects (Pitsikas *et al.* 2008; Hosseinzadel and Noraei 2009).

SAGE

Sage is another spice that has been used for thousands of years by Chinese medicine practitioners, Indian physicians, healers in ancient Greece, and by Native-American tribes, and is now being studied for its ability to improve mood and reduce anxiety.

Herbs As Medicine

Many panic sufferers want more than behavioral techniques alone. Maybe they've chosen the "no medication" route but don't yet trust their ability to relax and aren't ready, willing, or able to use food as medicine. They're still complaining of panic and anxiety despite use of supplemental vitamins, minerals, and fish oils. Consider the use of herbs as the next step in the treatment plan.

Herbs cannot be recommended halfheartedly. To ensure proper compliance, recommendations need to be conveyed with enthusiasm and must be specific as to how much to take, when to take it, how to take it (e.g. as a tea, liquid, capsule), which brand to get, and what side effects exist. First, assess your own personal comfort level. Do you have enough knowledge and experience to recommend specific herbs? Is prescribing herbs compatible with your license to practice? If you're experiencing any anxiety just thinking about these issues, then refer the client to a qualified herbalist. Whether you're prescribing yourself or making a referral, do so with conviction. Healing begins the moment someone hears your confidence about what you're prescribing, whether it's a specific herb, a healing food, a relaxation technique, or referral to another practitioner. Any personal doubts influence the outcome.

Because I have limited training in herbal medicine, I'm only comfortable with recommending the mildest herbs with the strongest safety records. Herbs can be purchased in bulk from reputable sources and then made into a tea, the gentlest delivery form. Liquid extracts are another good option as dosage can be easily manipulated. Because quality and potency vary significantly amongst the various manufacturers, always recommend a standardized preparation from a trusted company.

Learning about herb–drug interaction effects is crucial and as with prescription medications, the same precautions regarding pregnancy must be taken into consideration. Some people might be intolerant of various herbs and spices. Therefore, testing for food sensitivities, which would identify any problems, would be useful.

Reducing Anxiety

The following herbs to consider for reducing anxiety are given in order of preference. Sample them yourself before recommending them to someone else.

LEMON BALM

Referred to as the "gladden herb," lemon balm is a mild anxiolytic that helps with restlessness and agitation, and can also enhance mood. Because most of the beneficial features come from the essential oils, a tea made from fresh leaves works best. Homegrown lemon balm, which grows well in partial sunlight, offers more potency than store-bought. Gather lemon balm before it flowers to preserve the fragrant, lemony taste and avoid bitterness. To prepare, add a handful of fresh or dried leaves to one cup of boiling water, let it steep for about five to ten minutes and strain. If a liquid tincture is preferred, the standard recommendation is one to five droppers up to three times a day.

Lemon balm can be taken at bedtime for insomnia but doesn't induce sleepiness if taken during the day. If you're feeling stressed and anxious, the ritual of preparing and drinking lemon balm tea offers a soothing distraction. Just smelling the citrus scent can produce a relaxation effect.

PASSIONFLOWER

Passionflower is a natural, mild sedative that may be particularly helpful for those who can't fall asleep due to racing thoughts. The typical recommended dosage is one dropperful of a tincture in a little warm water, or two capsules of the extract, up to four times a day as needed. Passionflower is considered safe to use for children but should be avoided during pregnancy.

SKULLCAP

A delicate wildflower, skullcap has been used for centuries to induce a relaxed state. Although bitter, it can be prepared as a tea (try blending with mint to mask the taste) or taken as a tincture or capsule. Although considered safe for children, skullcap has been reported to be sedating, especially for those with depression in addition to anxiety.

Because passionflower combines well with skullcap and lemon balm, consider recommending this combination for reducing panic sensations. In her article "Herbs for the Anxious," published in *The Herb Quarterly*, Maria Noel Groves suggests blending these herbs for a soothing tea: Combine equal parts of dried passionflower, skullcap, lemon balm, and spearmint (for flavor) and steep one tablespoon of this mixture for 15 minutes in one cup of hot water. Strain well (Groves 2011). If making this tea during daytime hours, use less passionflower and skullcap, as they're more sedating than lemon balm.

MOTHERWORT

This herb offers fast relief from panic attacks, as it calms a rapid heartbeat. While kava (see below) only grows in tropical climates, motherwort grows easily in most gardens. Unfortunately, it's very bitter as a tea but can be blended with other herbs. Motherwort should not be used during pregnancy.

HOPS

Used to brew beer since the 11th century in Europe, hops act as a sedative and anxiolytic that can both induce sleep and improve the quality of sleep. It's typically combined with valerian.

KAVA

Kava is native to the South Pacific, where it was traditionally used as an intoxicating herb for ceremonies. Natives of this region used kava tea for centuries to promote relaxation, as in small doses it produces a quieting effect and acts as a muscle relaxant. Taken as a fresh root tincture, a fast-acting form, it usually has noticeable effects within minutes. As with lemon balm, kava doesn't have a sedative effect when taken during the day, but can promote sleep when taken at bedtime.

This herb got a bad reputation when reports of liver toxicity surfaced several years ago. However, the problem developed because some manufacturers, eager to cut costs, used the above ground parts of kava in their preparations rather than the root. Make sure you purchase kava root, not just kava, and only buy from a reputable supplier.

Although not considered to be addictive, little is known about its long-term effects; therefore kava should only be used for short-term support (not longer than three months at a time) and preferably on an intermittent rather than a daily basis. The usual recommendation is one dropperful of liquid tincture in warm water as needed, up to three times a day. As with other herbs, it should not be taken with alcohol, during pregnancy, or if liver diseases are present.

VALERIAN

Popular as far back as Roman times, valerian was known for both its anxiety-reducing and sleep-inducing properties. It's not recommended for children, should not be taken during pregnancy and should not be combined with alcohol, sedatives or antidepressant medications.

Adaptogens

Adaptogens are a class of herbs that have been used for thousands of years to reduce the effects of chronic stress and restore balance to the adrenal glands. In short, adaptogens help the body adapt to stress. All adaptogens are relatively safe, with no evidence of toxicity, but, as with any substance, can be harmful if misused or taken in extremely high doses.

Perhaps the most well known are the ginsengs: Asian or Panax ginseng, American ginseng and Siberian ginseng. These herbs help the body fight fatigue and physical exhaustion due to chronic stress, but because they may increase cortisol levels, they may be contraindicated for acute anxiety.

Many adaptogens come from Ayurvedic medicine, a 5000-year-old Indian healing system loosely translated from Sanskrit as "life knowledge or science." According to Ayurvedic tradition, "what heals also prevents." Herbs effective in treating specific conditions can also serve as a "food," providing targeted nourishment to specific physiological systems. For example, turmeric, popularized for its anti-inflammatory properties, can also be eaten as a culinary spice.

Adaptogens typically have multiple rather than single effects and are seldom used in isolation. Instead, they're combined in formulas designed to balance and harmonize the properties of the constituent herbs. Pairing of herbs illustrates the concept of synergy, as each may have a mild effect, but two or three together act more effectively to create change. Because ashwagandha, gotu kola and holy basil provide "calm energy," they work well for those who complain of feeling drained and exhausted due to their anxiety. Other adaptogens which may provide relief from anxiety are schisandra, reishi, and jiaogulan, herbs that have been used for centuries in Asia, and blue vervain, a little-known herb that can be combined with motherwort (one part blue vervain to two parts motherwort), skullcap, or ashwagandha. For a complete discussion of these and other adaptogens, one of the best guides to refer to is *Adaptogens: Herbs for Strength, Stamina, and Stress Relief* by David Winston and Steven Maimes (2007).

ASHWAGANDHA

Loosely translated as "strength of a horse" and sometimes referred to as Indian ginseng, ashwagandha increases energy and stamina while also promoting a calming and muscle-relaxing effect. It can be a good choice for those suffering from a combination of chronic anxiety, fatigue, and insomnia. While there are no reports of adverse side effects, it shouldn't be combined with alcohol and other sedatives or taken during pregnancy.

Ashwagandha is typically recommended in doses of 500 mg once or twice daily, before meals. As with all herbs, start with the smallest dose and work up gradually. Responses are typically seen within two to four weeks of regular use.

HOLY BASIL

Also referred to as tulsi, holy basil can restore balance to the adrenal glands. In India, expect to find holy basil growing in the garden of every family that practices Ayurvedic healing.

GOTU KOLA

Gotu kola has been used for hundreds of years in Indian and Chinese medicine and can reduce symptoms of stress, anxiety, and depression. Although it may help curb food cravings and urges to binge associated with stress, it may raise blood sugar levels.

PANAX GINSENG

This adaptogen increases energy and the ability to deal with stress. Although generally considered to be safe, it's not recommended for individuals with hypertension or hypoglycemia. Continuous use for more than about three months is also contraindicated.

Other Supplements to Consider

MELATONIN

Melatonin, a hormone produced in the pineal gland of the brain from the amino acid tryptophan, helps regulate sleep/wake cycles. Levels should be lowest during midday and highest at night, as daylight slows production, while darkness increases it. Melatonin levels decrease with age. Taking 1–5 mg about one hour before bedtime helps with sleep-onset insomnia and improves quality of sleep. The slow-release form may help prevent awakening in the middle of the night.

L-THEANINE

An amino acid found in the leaves of green tea, l-theanine is known for its relaxation-inducing effects and can also be used at night to promote sleep. Considered safe, it's usually recommended in dosages of up to 200 mg. per day, the equivalent of about four cups of green tea.

GABA

People with panic may have low levels of GABA, an inhibitory neurotransmitter. Although GABA is available in supplement form, adding the necessary raw materials to the diet can raise levels. The amino acid taurine, l-theanine, B3, B6, B12, the B vitamin inositol and magnesium boost GABA production.

A Final Word

Preparing healing foods or relaxing teas, experimenting with new spices, focusing on eliminating food triggers and environmental toxins, or obtaining herbal preparations all have some elements in common. These actions are proactive and can distract from anxiety. Panic sufferers often desire the security of having an anti-anxiety medication handy. Just knowing that relief awaits them in handy pill form creates a calming effect. The "medications" described in this chapter can serve that function just as well, if both therapist and client are sold on their value.

CHAPTER 10

Can Panic Go Away Without Medication?

"Spring comes, and the grass grows by itself."
—Japanese haiku

Applying an integrative, functional medicine model to understanding and managing panic disorder has the potential to balance brain chemistry and create profound and permanent changes. However, before addressing the question of whether or not panic will ever "just go away," let's turn to the elephant in the room that hasn't received much attention in this book: medication. Chances are your clients are either on medication for anxiety, have considered this option, or have been told by someone, typically their primary care doctor or psychiatrist, that they need an anti-anxiety medication. They may fear withdrawing or may wonder if they will be okay in the long run without it.

Wear Water Wings Forever or Learn to Swim

Here's how I explain medication to my patients:

Imagine young children who don't yet know how to swim. In order to be safe while in the water, they wear a flotation device around their upper arms commonly referred to as "water wings." Water wings enable a non-swimmer to get in the water and stay safe. What happens when children learn to swim? Sometimes they take off like guppies and no longer need their water wings. Some children like the security of the water wings, so the air is let out gradually until they feel confident enough to swim on their own. Anti-anxiety medications are like water wings. If the panic is preventing you from "getting into the pool," then by all means get a prescription. But here's something to think about: Do you want to be wearing water wings for the rest of your life, or do you want to learn to swim? Learning to quiet your mind and body, with the help of the right nutrients, is like learning how to swim.

You can take this analogy even further:

Medications lose their effectiveness the longer you take them. Sometimes you may need to take higher doses to get the same effect. That's like needing bigger and bigger water wings. Sometimes you may need to add a second drug. That's like having to wear an inner tube in addition to the water wings. Medications often have side effects. That's like getting a skin irritation from the water wings. Sometimes you may worry about running out of medication or not having any with you. That's like having to make sure you never set off for the pool or beach without the flotation device. Medications may not always work. That's like having to deal with torn or leaky water wings.

Now let's think about the process of learning how to swim. It's scary at first to come away from the edge of the pool and lift your feet off the bottom. It takes an encouraging teacher. It involves thinking to yourself: "I can do it!" Once you find yourself floating or dog paddling, the rest is just refining the process, learning new strokes, and practicing.

As you practice over and over, swimming becomes automatic. You're able to get in the pool and glide through the water without thinking about the mechanics of each stroke. Your brain's neural pathways know the movements. Each time you get in the pool, you don't think to yourself: "Will I know how to swim today?" or "What if I can't swim today and need water wings?"

Similarly, when you learn mind and body relaxation techniques for stopping panic and anxiety, it'll be challenging at first and you may be scared that they won't work for you. But if you keep practicing over and over, new pathways form in your brain so that stopping a panic attack becomes automatic. In fact, you won't feel panicky because you'll be used to a new way of being. You won't "get in the pool and forget how to swim." The body will know how to maintain a quiet state because of all that practice. You'll feel confident because you "know how to swim."

Practice Leads to Permanent Change

Reliance on medication may reinforce the belief that anxiety is a permanent condition; therefore expecting physical transformations through self-regulation equates to an exercise in futility. Why bother working so hard to relax when quick relief comes from swallowing a pill? The answer to that question can be found by turning to the science of hope: the study of neuroplasticity, cell turnover, and gene expression.

Neurologist Dr. David Perlmutter talks about neural networks as plastic, dynamic architecture, a constellation of neurons that light up momentarily to perform a specific task. When generating a specific thought, correlating neural networks are reinforced. For a more in-depth discussion of this fascinating topic, refer to his book *Power Up Your Brain* (Perlmutter and Villoldo 2011).

How does the workings of neural networks relate to panic disorder? When we engage in the same bad habits over and over again, neural pathways are reinforced over and over again. Consider the probability that if someone frequently experiences panic and anxiety becomes a way of life, the brain grows accustomed to these states. With each new fear-producing episode, that specific neural network strengthens, so the toxic thoughts and emotions, as well as the panic reaction associated with that network, become more entrenched as well.

Rewire Your Brain

Neuroscience research demonstrates that you can grow new brain cells and actually change the neural networks, as the human brain has the ability to rewire itself and form new connections between neurons. Neuroplasticity, the term used to describe the brain's ability to create new neural networks, means that the brain is capable of change and continues to change throughout life.

It's possible to alter brain function so as to permanently let go of panic. By not activating the circuitry currently associated with the panic response, the brain will stop using those networks. Rather than reinforcing the anxiety pathways, you can build the neural pathways for joy and inner quiet and express the genes associated with health and wellbeing. How does this happen?

Rewiring the brain's circuitry and creating positive neural pathways involves applying the integrative model I've presented. Specifically, enhance brain health with diet and lifestyle changes, and practice good breathing, positive thoughts, and positive imagery. New neural networks are strengthened by focused, sustained attention. It's not enough just to dabble in active stimulation; building new pathways requires continual practice. Think of how you master any skill, such as learning to play the piano. No one becomes an accomplished pianist by sitting down at the piano a couple of times. No one learns a piece of music by getting partway through and then walking away. Yet that's how many people approach mastering panic and anxiety; they may practice on a few occasions and conclude "it's not working" or begin to practice, give up, and go for the pill.

In addition to creating new neural pathways, the brain can grow new neurons, a process known as neurogenesis. Due to cell turnover, dying cells are replaced with new neurons. The brain constantly replenishes itself with new stem cells that can be converted into fully functional brain cells. Brain-derived neurotrophic factor (BDNF) plays a key role in neurogenesis. Among the factors that influence DNA to produce this protein are exercise that's perceived as enjoyable, meditation, reduced caloric intake, mental stimulation, and docosaheyaenic acid (DHA), a component of fish oil.

Studies on meditation demonstrate that it changes both the structure and function of the brain. In their book *How God Changes Your Brain,* Dr. Andrew Newberg and Mark Robert Waldman use brain mapping and imaging to show that meditation enhances blood flow, as well as function in the anterior cingulate. This brain region facilitates communication between the amygdala, the primitive brain structure associated with fear, and the prefrontal cortex. Meditation strengthens the anterior cingulate while quieting the amygdala, thus reducing the fear response and increasing reasoning. Irrational self-talk can convert to a rational inner voice. So once again, new ways of being can replace bad habits (Newberg and Waldman 2010).

Full mental engagement, or mindfulness, stimulates neurogenesis and strengthens the neural pathways that bring about positive changes. Permanent change also requires patience as well as diligent practice. Some changes will be observed immediately, but others may not appear until six months to a year from now or even longer. If everything changes and change can be viewed as a lifelong process, then it's possible to view oneself as on a continual path of transformation. Convey to clients the hopeful message that yes, they can even transform their genes. While the genetic code doesn't change, genetic expression does. Genes receive signals to turn on or off. Anxiety may "run in the family," but whether it's expressed depends on current lifestyle factors. Yes, my mother was a chronic worrier; so were both of my grandmothers, as well as my maternal aunt. But none of them knew how to take slow belly breaths or change their catastrophic thinking. They didn't practice yoga or meditate, and they didn't use food as medicine. Just because anxiety "runs in the family," it's not my destiny.

Do No Harm

Neuroplasticity, neurogenesis, and gene expression all suggest that the brain can change in positive ways, but are the strategies I've presented the right ones to create that change? How do we know if what we're recommending really works?

About 25 years ago, I arranged a meeting with a prominent cardiologist to present the benefits of relaxation training for anxiety in hopes of getting referrals from his practice. About ten minutes into the discussion, he asked to see the peer-reviewed, double blind, placebo-controlled studies conducted on large numbers of subjects and published in well-respected medical journals like the ones stacked on his desk. Not even waiting for my answer, he stood up and ended the meeting. I still remember his words: "Shame on you, a graduate of Northwestern University peddling this pseudoscience."

The kinds of studies that this physician wanted didn't exist at the time. Even today, behavioral research can't compete with the rigorous studies on medication for a number of reasons. Who's going to fund this type of research? I don't know of any company sending out a sales team to market breathing to physicians. Even if a study could be funded, finding large populations to participate in controlled behavioral research would be challenging. Furthermore, how would the investigators tease out what variable was responsible for the positive change? Like baking a cake, all ingredients must be present to produce a good outcome. Studying each factor in isolation doesn't work and represents another example of the reductionist thinking that defies the tenets of functional medicine. Rather than attempting to find the one remedy that's best for a particular condition, develop a unique plan for each unique individual.

My purpose in writing this book was to provide a guidebook and not a scholarly review of the research literature. Even if I documented all of the studies to date, the evidence probably wouldn't satisfy the skeptics like the physician described above. Hopefully, better research will be available in the near future, but I've been practicing integrative psychology for over 35 years and have yet to see it. Even if good scientific evidence from well-controlled studies existed, so what? A particular approach might not be right for everyone. The best evidence comes from your own research involving only one subject: the person who comes into your office seeking help.

Based on a sliding scale of evidence, the philosophy and techniques presented here don't need rigorous scientific studies to determine their safety and effectiveness. It's okay to recommend them because you're adhering to the first rule of healthcare: Do no harm. For example, when teaching slow, abdominal breathing, what's the potential for harm? Maybe someone complains of feeling dizzy or light-headed, but if so, you explain that those sensations are very normal and go away with continued practice. What's the potential for harm when reinforcing the use of rational thinking, positive imagery, or muscle relaxation? Any negative ramifications can be addressed and used to further learning.

The potential for harm increases when recommending yoga or vigorous exercise, but knowledge of the appropriate precautions and contraindications limits the risks. When applied to dietary recommendations, the "Do no harm" guideline may require a higher standard of proof. There's minimal risk when advising someone to cut down on sugar or caffeine, but prescribing supplements is another matter. Keep abreast of current research, stick with evidence-based protocols, be aware of any drug–supplement interaction effects, and refer to a qualified nutritionist or herbalist if you don't possess appropriate training in this area.

Because medications have documented side effects, including robbing the body of essential nutrients, the potential for harm is greatest when considering drug intervention. Therefore, the sliding scale of evidence demands the most rigorous controlled studies. If needed, use prescription medications as short-term "water wings" while helping clients take those first steps towards swimming on their own. Positive emotions, thoughts, behaviors, and food are some of the powerful new "medicines" that will help them move with ease through any rough waters ahead.

Filling a Medicine Chest to Build Resilience

Imagine building neural pathways, creating brain cells and promoting the expression of beneficial genes. What would that new superhighway look like? What words come to mind to describe it? How about resilience and hardiness?

Personal stories involving triumph over panic showcase heroic actions as great as depicted in epic novels. Over the years, I've been privileged to witness many such journeys and transformations from fearfulness to hardiness. One that comes to mind begins with a young high school girl who suffered from panic. Now an adult with a family and successful career, she recently completed a grueling triathlon and wrote an email to me in which she shared the process of finding mindfulness during the event. See how many coping strategies you can identify in her story:

> Given the metaphor of Triathlon as life, I think you'll be quite pleased with this race report. I have you to thank for many of the techniques I employed and thus I wanted to share it with you:

> I left the hotel and walked, happily, down to the swim start. It was really windy. The normally calm harbor was choppy and wavy. But into 74-degree water I went and prepared to start. The southbound leg was awesome. It felt like I was swimming with flippers. Then it hit me—I gotta swim upstream after the turn. Okay, no matter, today is about mental strength—"WHAT ARE YOU DOING AT THIS EXACT MOMENT?" So I enjoyed the fast warm up. Heading into the wind was a different story…at this point the harbor had no wind protection from the open water, no jetties or sea walls, no boats. It was wavy, choppy, chaotic and overwhelming. Nevertheless, I kept looking at the beautiful buildings against the blue sky and thinking what a privilege it was to be able to swim with this kind of backdrop. I found a "buddy" to pace with and finished the swim.

> The whole time while biking I was thinking to myself, "Right now—I feel strong. Right now—I feel fast. Right now—I feel my legs working. The run… Now,

I played a little mind trick on myself. I set my gauge to read ONLY the distance and the total elapsed time. That way I couldn't stress about pace or mph or heart rate. As usual my legs were sluggish, but I wasn't in pain and I wasn't feeling dead (this is all the "what are you feeling NOW" stuff). So I figured I'd run to the port-a-potties and see how I felt. I saw them—I felt good so I figured I'd run to the next ones. I saw them—I felt my legs starting to loosen and whoa—there's the first mile marker… I went on this way until the turn around. Now I really needed to dig deep if I had any chance of accomplishing my goal of a strong run finish. I counted how many steps it was from one landmark to the next (I guessed it would be 500—it was 503ish). That made me chuckle and whoa—there's the mile 5 marker. It's gonna be okay. I can run 1.2 miles—that's like 1000ish steps. Then someone coming the other direction let out a huge burp, which made me really made me chuckle and whoa there's the 6 mile marker. Now I had to get creative… So… I said, "See if you can count 5 dogs along the course before you finish." Yep that's right, I was countin' pups!…and whoa—there's the finishing mat… "THIS IS SO FUN!" Yippee!!

I think the major take away I have from this is I never thought about who was passing me or how far behind or ahead I was. I worked really hard to stay in the moment. What it allowed me to do was REALLY enjoy the experience of racing in the city that I love.

Just like a hardy plant that won't get blown over by a strong wind, hardy individuals withstand whatever stressor comes their way. Resiliency, which trumps fearfulness and panic, can be cultivated. All you need is possession of the right tools. Think of these tools as powerful medicine, and with sustained, regular use, the structure and functioning of the brain changes in profound ways. Pick and choose which ones to apply at any given time.

What would a well-equipped "medicine chest" contain?

- A hopeful message from healthcare professionals and loved ones that change is possible.

- Understanding that panic isn't a mental or physical illness.
- Knowing the workings of the fight-or-flight alarm system.
- Trusting that the relaxation response can be reawakened and strengthened to balance the stress response.
- Abdominal breathing at a rate of about five to six breathes per minute.
- Imagining positive sights, sounds, or physical sensations.
- Warming the heart with warm emotions, particularly gratitude.
- Rational thoughts.
- Muscle release and relaxation.
- Standing tall.
- Plenty of enjoyable movement and exercise.
- Belly laughter.
- Full engagement in mentally stimulating activities.
- Meaningful social connections.
- Mindfulness.
- Meditation.
- Yoga.
- Healing foods, especially the leaves of plants, plenty of protein from good sources, and healthy oils.
- The right supplements, especially vitamin D, B vitamins, omega-3 fish oils, and magnesium.
- Calming herbs as needed.
- Seven to eight hours of sleep each night.
- Patience.
- An intention to practice these strategies throughout the day, each and every day.
- Accepting whatever comes, including panic and anxiety.

What should be discarded?

- The terms "mental illness" *and* "mental disorder."

- The belief that medication or long-term psychotherapy is necessary.

- Toxic, irrational thoughts, particularly those that begin with "what if?"

- Pessimism about the potential for change.

- Guilt, judgment, and self-blame.

- Sugar.

- Caffeine.

- Environmental toxins.

- Highly processed foods.

- Impatience.

- Demand for change.

When to open the "medicine chest"

Many people prevent the onset of panic just knowing that they have an anti-anxiety pill with them to use if necessary. Similarly, true hardiness develops with awareness that internal control exists. As you reinforce this premise with others, simultaneously access your own internal resiliency. Knowing that you possess the right tools brings empowerment. Access them anytime, anywhere, and any place. Use them when life is good and when times are hard. Call on them as soon as you notice anxiety or panic sensations starting to grow. Most importantly, having learned "to swim," take the plunge into the deep end of the pool; in other words, face your fears. Repeatedly approach the panic sensations head on in order to practice a different way of being. This message can be imparted in many ways and at many stages along the journey.

Each practice offers new opportunities for focused attention on something good. Maybe it's a regularly scheduled five-minute breathing break several times a day. Perhaps for one minute every hour you find good postural alignment and do some shoulder rolls paired with slow, abdominal breathing. How about adding some laughter along with warm heart-centered emotions to a busy day? Maybe one or two yoga poses serve as mini-breaks or a daily practice for 20–30 minutes can be woven into the day. Can you try some green tea instead of coffee, start the day with protein, or add a green vegetable to your dinner plate? But of all the tools available, the best one may be what's most difficult to come to terms with: accepting panic and anxiety.

The Most Important Tool: Accepting the "Full Catastrophe"

Jon Kabat-Zinn (1990) chose to title his book *Full Catastrophe Living* because it implies an appreciation for the full richness of life, both the joys and the sorrows. By successfully coping with life's difficulties and using obstacles to find strength and wisdom, you're embracing "the full catastrophe" and building hardiness. Implicit in accepting the negatives along with the positives is the abandonment of impossible standards. As a therapist, that means accepting that some people won't get better, some might take a little longer, and some may choose medication over your treatment plan. For a parent, that means fully accepting how your child functions at this point in time rather than demanding change.

Rather than viewing panic as a negative, view it as a positive and encourage others to do so as well: an opportunity to practice mindfulness and accept all of life's experiences, gain a better self-perception, laugh at yourself, find balance, and foster greater resilience. Look back on panic attacks and see them as the vehicles that brought you into a state of good health.

Whether you picked up this book because you treat panic disorder, care for someone who has panic attacks, or have experienced them yourself, use the "medicine chest" as a starting point for discovering balance, strength, and inner quiet, but view it as a work in progress. Trusting creativity and mindfulness, you'll continually find additional ways of creating internal stillness, both for yourself and someone you care for. The more you practice taking control of thoughts, perceptions, and bodily sensations, and the more you add good food and positive connections to your life, the greater the opportunity for achieving a state of harmony. Above all, don't forget to breathe.

Resources

Acceptance

Books

Kitchen Table Wisdom. Naomi Rachel Remen, M.D. (1996) Riverhead Books.

Adrenal Fatigue

Books

Are You Tired and Wired? Marcelle Pick (2011) Hay House.

Anxiety and Panic

Books

Don't Panic. Reid Wilson (1986) Harper and Row.

Peace from Nervous Suffering. Claire Weeks (1978) Bantam.

The Panic Attack Recovery Book. Shirley Swede and Seymour Jaffe (2000) New American Library.

Triumph over Fear. Jerilyn Ross (1994) Bantam.

Organizations

Anxiety Disorders Association of America
www.adaa.com

Anxiety Disorders Association of Canada
www.anxietycanada.ca

Anxiety Treatment Australia
www.anxietyaustralia.com.au

Anxiety UK
www.anxietyuk.org.uk

International Association of Anxiety Disorders
www.iaod.org

Websites

Healthy Place (America's mental health channel)

www.healthyplace.com/anxiety-panic/menu-id-69

The Anxiety Panic internet resource (tAPir)

http://algy.com

Autism

Organizations

Autism Canada Foundation
www.autismcanada.org

Autism Research Institute [US]
www.autism.com

Resources for Autism [UK]
www.resourcesforautism.org.uk

Ayurvedic Medicine

Books

Ayurveda. Todd Caldecott (2006) Mosby.

Biofeedback

Books

The HeartMath Solution. Doc Childre and Howard Martin with Donna Beech (2000) HarperCollins.

Transforming Anxiety. Doc Childre and Deborah Rozman (2006) New Harbinger Publications.

Transforming Stress. Doc Childre and Deborah Rozman (2005) New Harbinger Publications.

Organizations

Association for Applied Psychophysiology and Biofeedback [US]
www.aapb.org

Biofeedback Certification Institute of America
www.bcia.org

Biofeedback Foundation of Europe
www.bfe.org

Trainers for Paced Breathing
Emwave Personal Trainer: www.heartmath.com

Resperate: www.resperate.com

EZ Air Plus: www.BFE.org/breathpacer

Breathing

see also Biofeedback

Books

A Life Worth Breathing. Max Strom (2010) Skyhorse Publishing.

Breathe Well, Be Well. Robert Fried (1999) John Wiley & Sons.

The Breathing Book. Donna Farhi (1996) Henry Holt and Co.

CD recordings

Breathing: The Master Key to Self Healing. Andrew Weil, M.D. (1999) Sounds True.

Healthy Breathing: A Practical Course in Breathing Techniques to Rejuvenate and Transform Your Life. Ken Cohen (2005) Sounds True.

Cognitive Behavior Therapy

Books

A New Guide to Rational Living. Albert Ellis, Ph.D. (1975) Wilshire Book Company.

How to Control Your Anxiety Before It Controls You. Albert Ellis, Ph.D. (1998) Citadel Press.

Mastery of Your Anxiety and Panic. David Barlow and Michelle Craske (1989) Graywind Publications.

How to Stubbornly Refuse to Make Yourself Miserable about Anything. Albert Ellis, Ph.D. (2006) Citadel Press.

The Feeling Good Handbook. David Burns (2011) Penguin.

Distraction

Books

50 Ways to Soothe Yourself Without Food. Susan Albers, Psy.D. (2009) New Harbinger Publications.

Environmental Toxins

Books

Home Safe Home. Debra Lynn Dadd (1997) Tarcher/Putman.

Super Natural Home. Beth Greer (2009) Rodale Books.

Organizations

Environmental Working Group [US]
www.ewg.org

Exercise

Books

An Everyday Guide to Your Health. David Sobel and Mary Louise Hornbacher (1973) GrossmanPublishers/Viking Press.

Flow. Mihaly Csikszentmihalyi (1990) Harper Perennial.

The Chemistry of Joy. Henry Emmons and Rachel Kranz. (2006) Simon and Schuster.

Functional and Integrative Medicine

Books

Manifesto for a New Medicine. James Gordon, M.D. (1996) Perseus Books.

Spontaneous Healing. Andrew Weil, M.D. (2000) Ballantine.

Textbook of Functional Medicine. David S. Jones, M.D. (ed.) (2010) Institute for Functional Medicine.

UltraMind Solution. Mark Hyman, M.D. (2009) Scribner.

Unstuck. James Gordon (2008) Penguin.

Organizations

American Holistic Medical Association
www.holisticmedicine.org

Arizona Center for Integrative Medicine
http://integrativemedicine.arizona.edu

Australasian Integrative Medicine Association Inc.
www.aima.net.au

British College of Integrative Medicine
www.integrativemedicine.uk.com

British Society of Integrated Medicine
www.bsim.org.uk

Canadian Institute of Natural and Integrative Medicine
www.cinim.org

Center for Mind-Body Medicine [US]
www.cmbm.org

European Federation for Complementary and Alternative Medicine
www.efcam.eu

Institute for Functional Medicine [US]
www.functionalmedicine.org

UltraWellness Center [US]
www.ultrawellness.com

Websites

Dr. Andrew Weil's website
www.drweil.com

Dr. James Gordon's website
www.jamesgordonmd.com

Dr. Mark Hyman's website
www.drhyman.com

Humor

Organizations

American School of Laughter Yoga
www.laughteryogaamerica.com

Laughter Yoga International
www.laughteryoga.org

Website

AFI's 100 Years...100 Laughs (American Film Institute)
www.afi.com/100years/laughs.aspx

Films that Laugh at Anxiety

Analyze This (1999) Harold Ramis, Director

Annie Hall (1977) Woody Allen, Director

Broadcast News (1987) James L. Brooks, Director

High Anxiety (1977) Mel Brooks, Director

The 40-Year-Old Virgin (2005) Judd Apatow, Director

The Producers (1968) Mel Brooks, Director

What About Bob? (1991) Frank Oz, Director

Imagery

Books

30 Scripts for Relaxation Imagery and Inner Healing, Vol. 1. Julie T. Lusk (ed) (1992) Whole Person Associates.

Healing Spaces. Esther Sternberg, M.D. (2009) Belknap Press of Harvard University Press.

Staying Well with Guided Imagery. Belleruth Naparstek (1994) Warner Books.

Organizations

Academy for Guided Imagery [US]
www.acadgi.com

Imagery International
www.imageryinternational.org

Mindfulness/Meditation

Books

Full-Catastrophe Living. Jon Kabat-Zinn (1990) Dell.

Starbright: Meditations for Children. Maureen Garth (1991) HarperCollins.

Muscle Relaxation

Books

Autogenic Therapy. Wolfgang Luthe and Johannes Heinrich Schultz. (1969) Grune and Stratton.

Experiences in Visual Thinking. Robert McKim (1972) Brooks/Cole Publishing.

New Directions in Progressive Relaxation Training: A Guidebook for Helping Professionals. Douglas A. Berneteín, Thomas D. Berkovec and Holy Hazlett-Stevens (2000) Praeger.

Ready…Set…R.E.L.A.X.: A Research-Based Program of Relaxation, Learning and Self-Esteem for Children. Jeffrey S. Allen, M.Ed. and Roger J. Klein, Psy.D. (1997) Inner Coaching.

Relaxercise. David Zemach-Bersin, Kaethe Zemach-Bersin and Mark Reese. (1990) HarperCollins.

The Relaxation Response. Herbert Benson, M.D. (1975) William Morrow and Co.

Neuroplasticity and Neurogenesis

Books

Buddha's Brain. Rick Hanson with Richard Mendius (2009) New Harbinger Publications.

Power Up Your Brain. David Perlmutter, M.D. and Alberto Villoldo, Ph.D. (2011) Hay House.

Rewire Your Brain. John B. Arden, Ph.D. (2010) John Wiley and Sons.

Nutrition

Books

Clinical Nutrition. DaAnn Liska, Ph.D., *et al.* (2004) Institute for Functional Medicine.

Digestive Wellness (4th edn). Elizabeth Lipski, Ph.D., CCN, CHN. (2012) McGraw-Hill.

Healing Spices. Bharat Aggarwal with Debora Yost (2011) Sterling Publishing.

Herb, Nutrient, and Drug Interactions. Mitchell Bebel Stargrove, Jonathan Treasure and Dwight L. McKee. (2008) Mosby Elsevier.

Sugar Shock. Connie Bennett and Stephen Sinatra (2006) Berkley Publishing Group.

The Inside Tract: Your Good Gut Guide to Great Digestive Health. Gerald E. Mullin, M.D. and Kathie Madonna Swift, MS, RD, LDN. (2011) Rodale.

Organizations

American Botanical Council
www.herbalgram.org

American Herbalist Guild
www.americanherbalistsguild.com

Herb Research Foundation [US]
www.herbs.org

The Herbal Society [UK]
www.herbsociety.org.uk

International and American Associations of Clinical Nutritionists
www.iaacn.org

Panic

see Anxiety and Panic

Stress Response

Books

Mind as Healer, Mind as Slayer. Kenneth Pelletier (1977) Dell Publishing.

The Stress of Life. Hans Selye (1978) McGraw-Hill.

Why Zebras Don't Get Ulcers. Robert Sapolsky (2004) St. Martin's Griffin.

Yoga

Books

Integrated Yoga. Nicole Cuomo (1997) Jessica Kingsley Publishers.

Light on Yoga. B.K.S. Iyengar (1976) Schocken Books.

Relax and Renew. Judith Lasater (1995) Rodmell Press.

Yoga for Children with Autism Spectrum Disorders. Dion W. Betts and Stacey Betts (2006) Jessica Kingsley Publishers.

Yoga for Depression. Amy Weintraub (2004) Broadway Books.

Yoga Therapy for Every Special Child. Nancy Williams (2010) Singing Dragon.

Websites

Yoga Finder
www.yogafinder.com

Yoga Journal
www.yogajournal.com

Green Smoothie Recipe

Green smoothies are a great way to incorporate dark, leafy greens into the diet. They are quick and easy to prepare, and all you need is a kitchen blender. Begin with the milder greens and add more fruit if necessary.

Ingredients for my favorite green smoothie recipe:

1 cup (240 ml) water or unsweetened almond milk

1 cup (240 ml) dark leafy greens, e.g. romaine or other dark lettuce leaves, spinach, kale (tear off from center stem), parsley, collards, Swiss chard, dandelion. Try to rotate the choice of greens. Lettuce and spinach are the mildest tasting.

1 cup (240 ml) fruit (either fresh or frozen, preferably organic), e.g. blueberries, raspberries, strawberries, banana, mango, melon. Avoid banana, mango, and other tropical fruit if you have problems with blood sugar control.

½ of an avocado and/or 1 tablespoon (15ml) nut butter (preferably almond, hazelnut, or cashew)

1 serving of protein powder (optional), e.g. hemp protein, brown rice protein, pea protein, whey protein

1 tablespoon (15ml) ground flaxseed (optional)

ice (optional)

Place all ingredients in a blender and mix until smooth and creamy. If you're not using a high-powered blender, the mixture may need to be poured through a fine strainer before drinking.

Bibliography

Aggarwal, B.B. (2011) *Healing Spices: How to Use 50 Everyday and Exotic Spices to Boost Health and Beat Disease.* New York, NY: Sterling Publishing.

Albers, S.P. (2009) *50 Ways to Soothe Yourself Without Food.* Oakland, CA: New Harbinger Publications.

Allen, J.S. and Klein, R. (1997) *Ready... Set... R.E.L.A.X.: A Research-Based Program of Relaxation, Learning and Self-Esteem for Children.* Watertown, WI: Inner Coaching.

American Psychiatric Association. (2000) *Diagnostic and Statistical Manual of Mental Disorders DSM-IV-TR* (4th edn, text revision). Arlington, VA: American Psychiatric Association.

Arden, J.B. (2009) *Heal Your Anxiety Workbook.* Boston, MA: Fairwinds.

Arden, J.B. (2010) *Rewire Your Brain: Think Your Way to a Better Life.* Hoboken, NJ: John Wiley and Sons.

Barlow, D.H. and Craske, M.G. (1989) *Mastery of Your Anxiety and Panic.* Albany, NY: Graywind Publications.

Beck, A.T. (1976) *Cognitive Therapy and the Emotional Disorders.* New York, NY: New American Library.

Bennett, C. and Sinatra, S. (2006) *Sugar Shock: How Sweets and Simple Carbs Can Derail Your Life and How You Can Get Back on Track.* New York, NY: Berkley Publishing Group.

Benson, H.M. (1975) *The Relaxation Response.* New York, NY: William Morrow and Co.

Berik, P., Verdu, E.F., Foster, J.A., Marci, J., *et al.* (2010) "Chronic gastrointestinal inflammation induces anxiety-like behavior and alters central nervous system biochemistry in mice." *Gastroenterology 139,* 2102–2112.

Berk, L.S., Tan, S.A., Nehlsen-Cannrella, S., Napier, B.J., *et al.* (1988) "Humor-associated laughter decreases cortisol and increases spontaneous lymphocyte blastogenesis." *Clinical Research 36,* 435A.

Bernstein, D. and Borkovec, T.D. (1973) *Progressive Relaxation Training: A Manual for the Helping Professions.* Champaign, IL: Research Press.

Bernstein, D. and Borkovec, T.D. (2000) *New Directions in Progressive Relaxation Training: A Guidebook for Helping Professionals.* Westport, CT: Praeger.

Betts, D.E. and Betts, S.W. (2006) *Yoga for Children with Autism Spectrum Disorders: A Step-by-Step Guide for Parents and Caregivers.* London: Jessica Kingsley Publishers.

Blake, R. (1987) *Mind over Medicine.* London: Pan Books.

Bloomfield, H.H. (1998) *Healing Anxiety with Herbs.* New York, NY: HarperCollins.

Bock, K.M. and Stauth, C.H. (2008) *Healing the New Childhood Epidemics: Autism, ADHD, Asthma, and Allergies: The Groundbreaking Program for the 4-A Disorders.* New York, NY: Ballantine Books.

Borysenko, J. (1988) *Minding the Body, Mending the Mind.* Toronto: Bantam Books.

Borysenko, J.P. and Borysenko, M. (1994) *The Power of the Mind to Heal.* Carson, CA: Hay House.

Bourne, E.J. (1990) *The Anxiety and Phobia Workbook.* Oakland, CA: New Harbinger Publications.

Bourne, E.J. (2004) *Natural Relief for Anxiety.* Oakland, CA: New Harbinger Publications.

Brach, T. (2003) *Radical Acceptance: Embracing Your Life with the Heart of the Buddha.* New York, NY: Bantam Books.

Bravo, J.A., Forsythe, P., Chew, M.V., Escaravage, E., *et al.* (2011) "Ingestion of *Lactobacillus* strain regulates emotional behavior and central GABA receptor expression in a mouse via the vagus nerve." *Proceedings of the National Academy of Sciences of the United States of America 108,* 16050–16055.

Brown, R.P., Gerberg, P., and Muskin, P.R. (2009) *How to Use Herbs, Nutrients and Yoga in Mental Health Care.* New York, NY: W.W. Norton and Co.

Brown, S. (2009) *Macrobiotics for Life: A Practical Guide to Healing for Body, Mind, and Heart.* Berkeley, CA: North Atlantic Books.

Burns, D.D. (1980) *Feeling Good: The New Mood Therapy.* New York, NY: Penguin Books.

Burns, D.D. (2011) *The Feeling Good Handbook.* New York, NY: Penguin Books.

Caldecott, T. (2006) *Ayurveda: The Divine Science of Life.* Edinburgh: Mosby.

Childre, D. and Martin, H. (2000) *The HeartMath Solution.* New York, NY: HarperCollins.

Childre, D. and Rozman, D. (2005) *Transforming Stress: The HeartMath Solution for Relieving Worry, Fatigue, and Tension.* Oakland, CA: New Harbinger Publications.

Childre, D. and Rozman, D. (2006) *Transforming Anxiety: The HeartMath Solution for Overcoming Fear and Worry and Creating Serenity.* Oakland, CA: New Harbinger Publications.

Chopra, D. (1989) *Quantum Healing.* New York, NY: Bantam Books.

Cousins, N. (1979) *Anatomy of an Illness As Perceived by the Patient: Reflections on Healing and Regeneration.* New York, NY: W. W. Norton and Co.

Cousins, N. (1983) *The Healing Heart.* New York, NY: W. W. Norton and Co.

Cousins, N. (1989) *Head First: The Biology of Hope.* New York, NY: E.P. Dutton.

Crook, W.G. (1999) *The Yeast Connection Handbook.* Jackson, TN: Professional Books.

Csikszentmihalyi, M. (1990) *Flow: The Psychology of Optimal Experience.* New York, NY: Harper Perennial.

Cuomo, N. (1997) *Integrated Yoga: Yoga with a Sensory Integrative Approach.* London: Jessica Kingsley Publishers.

Dadd, D.L. (1997) *Home Safe Home: Protecting Yourself and Your Family from Everyday Toxics and Harmful Household Products.* New York, NY: Tarcher/Putnam.

Davidson, R.J.-Z., Kabat-Zinn, J., Schumacher, J., Rosenkranz, M., *et al.* (2003) "Alterations in brain and immune function produced by mindfulness meditation." *Psychosomatic Medicine 65,* 564–570.

Davis, D.P. (2011) *Disconnect: The Truth about Cell Phone Radiation, What the Industry Is Doing to Hide It, and How to Protect Your Family.* New York, NY: Penguin Books.

Davis, M., Eshelman, E.R., and McKay, M. (2008) *The Relaxation and Stress Reduction Workbook* (6th edn). Oakland, CA: New Harbinger Publications.

DesMaisons, K. (1998) *Potatoes Not Prozac: A Natural Seven-Step Dietary Plan to Stabilize the Level of Sugar in Your Blood, Control Your Cravings and Lose Weight, and Recognize How Foods Affect the Way You Feel.* New York, NY: Simon and Schuster.

Dossey, L. (1989) *Recovering the Soul.* New York, NY: Bantam Books.

Ellis, A. (1977) *A Garland of Rational Songs.* New York, NY: Institute for Rational Emotive Therapy.

Ellis, A. (1998) *A New Guide to Rational Living.* Chatsworth, CA: Wilshire Book Company.

Ellis, A. (1998) *How to Control Your Anxiety Before It Controls You.* New York, NY: Citadel Press/Kensington Publishing.

Ellis, A. (2006) *How to Stubbornly Refuse to Make Yourself Miserable about Anything: Yes Anything!* (rev. edn) New York, NY: Citadel Press/Kensington Publishing.

Emmons, H.M. (2006) *The Chemistry of Joy: A Three-Step Program for Overcoming Depression Through Western Science and Eastern Wisdom.* New York, NY: Simon and Schuster.

Engelhart, T.W. (2007) *I Am Grateful: Recipes and Lifestyle of Cafe Gratitude.* Berkeley, CA: North Atlantic Books.

Epstein, S. (1967) "Toward a Unified Theory of Anxiety." In B. Maher (ed.) *Progress in Experimental Personality Research, Vol. 4.* New York, NY: Academic Press.

Farhi, D. (1996) *The Breathing Book: Good Health and Vitality Through Essential Breath Work.* New York, NY: Henry Holt and Co.

Flippin, R. (1992) "Slow Down, You Breathe Too Fast." *American Health XI*, 71–75.

Freeman, L.P. (1998) *Panic Free: Eliminate Anxiety/Panic Attacks Without Drugs and Take Control of Your Life.* Colorado Springs, CO: Health Wise Publications.

Fried, R. (1987) *The Hyperventilation Syndrome.* Baltimore, MD: Johns Hopkins University Press.

Fried, R. (1990) *The Breath Connection.* New York, NY: Plenum.

Fried, R. (1999) *Breathe Well, Be Well: A Program to Relieve Stress, Anxiety, Asthma, Hypertension, Migraine, and Other Disorders for Better Health.* New York, NY: John Wiley and Sons.

Fry, W.F. (1992) "The physiological effects of humor, mirth, and laughter." *Journal of the American Medical Association 267*, 4, 1874–1878.

Garth, M. (1991) *Starbright: Meditations for Children.* San Francisco, CA: HarperCollins.

Gawain, S. (2002) *Creative Visualization: Use the Power of Your Imagination to Create What You Want in Your Life.* Novato, CA: New World Library.

Gladwell, M. (2008) *Outliers: The Story of Success.* New York, NY: Little, Brown and Co.

Gordon, J.S. (1996) *Manifesto for a New Medicine: Your Guide to Healing Partnerships and the Wise Use of Alternative Therapies.* Reading MA: Perseus Books.

Gordon, J.S. (2008) *Unstuck: Your Guide to the Seven-Stage Journey out of Depression.* New York, NY: Penguin Books.

Green, E. and Green, A. (1977) *Beyond Biofeedback.* New York, NY: Dell Publishing.

Greer, B. (2009) *Super Natural Home: Improve Your Health, Home, and Planet – One Room at a Time.* New York, NY: Rodale Books.

Groves, M.N. (2011) "Herbs for the anxious." *The Herb Quarterly*, Spring, 22–23.

Hanh, T. (1976) *The Miracle of Mindfulness: A Manual on Meditation.* Boston, MA: Beacon Press.

Hanson, R.P. (2009) *Buddha's Brain: The Practical Neuroscience of Happiness, Love and Wisdom.* Oakland, CA: New Harbinger Publications.

Hauck, P.A. (1975) *Overcoming Worry and Fear.* Philadelphia, PA: Westminister Press.

Helgoe, L.A., Wilhelm, L.R. and Kommor, M.J. (2005) *The Anxiety Answer Book.* Naperville, IL: Sourcebooks.

Herbert, M.R. (2005) "Autism: A brain disorder, or a disorder that affects the brain?" *Clinical Neuropsychiatry 6*, 354–379.

Hosseinzadeh, H. and Noraei, N.B. (2009) "Anxiolytic and hypnotic effect of Crocus sativus aqueous extract and its constituents, crocin and safranal, in mice." *Phytotherapy Research 23*, 768–774.

Hyman, M. (2009) *The UltraMind Solution: The Simple Way to Defeat Depression, Overcome Anxiety, and Sharpen Your Mind.* New York, NY: Scribner.

Iyengar, B.K. (1976) *Light on Yoga* (rev. edn). New York, NY: Schocken Books.

Jacobson, E. (1929) *Progressive Relaxation.* Chicago, IL: University of Chicago Press.

Jones, D.S. (ed.) (2010) *Textbook of Functional Medicine.* Gig Harbor, WA: Institute for Functional Medicine.

Kabat-Zinn, J. (1990) *Full Catastrophe Living.* New York, NY: Dell Publishing.

Kalisch, R.W., Wiech, K., Critchley, H., Seymour, B., *et al.* (2005) "Anxiety reduction through detachment, subjective, physiological and neural effects." *Journal of Cognitive Neuroscience 17*, 874–883.

King, J.C. (1988) "Hyperventilation: A therapist's point of view." *Journal of the Royal Society of Medicine 81*, 532–536.

King, M.S., Stanley, G. and Burrows, G. (1987) *Stress: Theory and Practice.* Sydney, NSW: Grune and Stratton.

Kuhn, M.A. and Winston, D. (2008) *Herbal Therapy and Supplement: A Scientific and Traditional Approach.* Philadelphia, PA: Wolters Kluwer/Lippincott, Williams and Wilkins.

Lasater, J.P. (1995) *Relax and Renew: Restful Yoga for Stressful Times.* Berkeley, CA: Rodmell Press.

Lee, C. (2010) "Legs-up-the-wall pose." *Yoga Journal*, September, 70–75.

Lehrer, P.M., Woolfolk, R.I.., and Sime, W.E. (eds.) (2007) *Principles and Practice of Stress Management* (3rd edn). New York, NY: Guilford Press.

Leite, J.R., Scabra, Mde, L., Maluf, E, Assolant, K. *et al.* (1986) "Pharmacology of lemongrass (*Cymbopogon citratus* Stapt.). III. Assessment of eventual toxic hypnotic and axiolytic effects on humans." *Journal of Ethnopharmacology 17*, 75–83.

Leshan, L. (1974) *How to Meditate.* Boston, MA: Little, Brown and Co.

Ley, R. (1985) "Agoraphobia, the panic attack and the hyperventilation syndrome." *Behavior Research Therapy 23*, 79–81.

Lipski, E. (2012) *Digestive Wellness* (4th edn). New York, NY: McGraw Hill.

Liska, D., Quinn, S., Lukaczer, D., Jones, D.S., and Lerman, R.H. (2004) *Clinical Nutrition: A Functional Approach* (2nd edn). Gig Harbor, WA: Institute for Functional Medicine.

Lusk, J.T. (1992) *30 Scripts for Relaxation Imagery and Inner Healing, Vol. 1.* Duluth, MN: Whole Person Associates.

Lusk, J.T. (1993) *30 Scripts for Relaxation Imagery and Inner Healing, Vol. 2.* Duluth, MN: Whole Person Associates.

Luthe, W. and Schultz, J.H. (1969) *Autogenic Therapy.* New York, NY: Grune and Stratton.

McCall, T. (2007) *Yoga as Medicine: The Yogic Prescription for Health and Healing.* New York, NY: Bantam Books.

McKim, R.H. (1972) *Experiences in Visual Thinking.* Monterray, CA: Brooks/Cole Publishing.

Mahendra, P. and Bisht, S. (2011) "Anti-anxiety activity of *Coriandrum sativum* assessed using different experimental anxiety models." *Indian Journal of Pharmacology 43*, 574–577.

Meichenbaum, D. (1977) *Cognitive-Behavior Modification: An Integrative Approach*. New York, NY: Plenum Press.

Miehl-Madrona, L. (2010) *Healing the Mind Through the Power of Story: The Promise of Narrative Psychiatry*. Rochester, VT: Bear and Co.

Miller, F.L. (1999) *How to Calm Down: Three Deep Breaths to Peace of Mind*. New York, NY: Warner Books.

Moses, B. (1998) *It's All Well and Good: A Wholistic Guidebook to Relaxation and Wellness*. Bloomington, IN: Oh Well.

Mullin, G.E. and Swift, K.M. (2011) *The Inside Tract: Your Good Gut Guide to Great Digestive Health*. Emmaus, PA: Rodale.

Naparstek, B. (1994) *Staying Well with Guided Imagery: How to Harness the Power of Your Imagination for Health and Healing*. New York, NY: Warner Books.

Newberg, A. and Waldman, M.R. (2010) *How God Changes Your Brain*. New York, NY: Ballantine Books.

Nuernberger, P. (1981) *Freedom from Stress: A Holistic Approach*. Honesdale, PA: Himalayan International Institute of Yoga Science and Philosophy.

NurrieStearns, M. and NurrieStearns, R. (2010) *Yoga for Anxiety: Meditations and Practices for Calming the Body and Mind*. Oakland, CA: New Harbinger Publications.

Pelletier, K. (1977) *Mind as Healer, Mind as Slayer: A Holistic Approach to Preventing Stress Disorders*. New York, NY: Dell Publishing.

Peper, E. and Machose, M. (1993) "Symptom prescription: Inducing anxiety by 70% exhalation." *Biofeedback and Self-Regulation 18*, 3, 133–139.

Perlmutter, D.M. and Villoldo, A. (2011) *Power Up Your Brain: The Neuroscience of Enlightenment*. Carlsbad, CA: Hay House.

Pick, M. (2011) *Are You Tired and Wired? Your Proven 30-Day Program for Overcoming Adrenal Fatigue and Feeling Fantastic Again*. Carlsbad, CA: Hay House.

Pitsikas, N., Boultadakis, A., Georgiadou, G., Tarantilis, PA., and Sakellaridis, N. (2008) "Effects of the active constituents of Crocus sativus L., crocins, in an animal model of anxiety." *Phytomedicine 15*, 1135–1139.

Pollan, M. (2009) *Food Rules: An Eater's Manual*. New York, NY: Penguin Books.

Rama, S., Ballentine, R., and Hymes, A. (1979) *Science of Breath*. Honesdale, PA: The Himalayan International Institute of Yoga Science and Philosophy.

Remen, N.R. (1996) *Kitchen Table Wisdom: Stories That Heal*. New York, NY: Riverhead Books.

Roskies, E. (1987) *Stress Management for the Healthy Type A*. New York, NY: Guilford Press.

Ross, J. (1994) *Triumph over Fear: A Book of Help and Hope for People with Anxiety, Panic Attacks, and Phobias*. New York, NY: Bantam Books.

Sapolsky, R.M. (2004) *Why Zebras Don't Get Ulcers* (3rd edn). New York, NY: St. Martin's Griffin.

Schmidt, M. (2006) *Brain-Building Nutrition: How Dietary Fat and Oils Affect Mental, Physical, and Emotional Intelligence*. Berkeley, CA: Frog Books.

Selye, H. (1978) *The Stress of Life*. New York, NY: McGraw-Hill.

Servan-Schreiber, D. (2004) *The Instinct to Heal: Curing Depression, Anxiety, and Stress Without Drugs and Without Talk Therapy*. New York, NY: Rodale.

Sobel, D.S. and Hornbacher, F.L. (1973) *An Everyday Guide to Your Health*. New York, NY: Grossman Publishers/Viking Press.

Sonavane, G.S., Sarveeiya, V.P., Kasture, V.S., and Kasture, S.B. (2002) "Anxiogenic activity of *Myristica fragrans* seeds." *Pharmacological Biochemistry and Behaviour 71*, 230–244.

Stargrove, M.B, Treasure, J., and McKee, D.L. (2008) *Herb, Nutrient, and Drug Interactions: Clinical Implications and Therapeutic Strategies.* St. Louis, MO: Mosby Elsevier.

Sternberg, E. (2009) *Healing Spaces: The Science of Place and Well-Being.* Cambridge, MA: Belknap Press of Harvard University Press.

Strohle, A., Feller, C., Onken, M., Godemann, F., Heinz, A., and Dimeo, F. (2005) "The acute anti-panic activity of aerobic exercise." *American Journal of Psychiatry 162*, 2376–2378.

Strom, M. (2010) *A Life Worth Breathing: A Yoga Master's Handbook of Strength, Grace, and Healing.* New York, NY: Skyhorse Publishing.

Suzuki, S. and Dixon, T. (eds.) (1970) *Zen Mind, Beginner's Mind.* New York, NY: Weatherhill.

Swede, S. and Jaffe, S.S. (2000) *The Panic Attack Recovery Book: Step-by-Step Techniques to Reduce Anxiety and Change Your Life – Natural, Drug-Free, Fast Results.* New York, NY: New American Library/Penguin Books.

Talbott, S.M. (2002) *The Cortisol Connection: Why Stress Makes You Fat and Ruins Your Health – And What You Can Do About It.* Alameda, CA: Hunter House.

Taylor, S.E., Klein, L.C., Lewis, B.P., Gruenewald, T.L., *et al.* (2000) "Behavioral responses to stress in females: Tend-and-befriend, not fight-or-flight." *Psychological Review 107*, 411–429.

Weekes, C. (1978) *Peace from Nervous Suffering.* New York, NY: Bantam Books.

Weil, A. (1995) *Spontaneous Healing: How to Discover and Embrace Your Body's Natural Ability to Maintain and Heal Itself.* New York, NY: Ballantine Books/Random House.

Weil, A. (2010) *The Need for a New Paradigm of Mental Health.* Opening Address at the Integrative Mental Health Conference, University of Arizona, Tuscon.

Weil, A. (2011) *Spontaneous Happiness.* New York, NY: Little, Brown and Co.

Weinstock, L. and Gilman, F. (1998) *Overcoming Panic Disorder: A Woman's Guide.* Lincolnwood, IL: Contemporary Books.

Weintraub, A. (2004) *Yoga for Depression: A Compassionate Guide to Relieve Suffering Through Yoga.* New York, NY: Broadway Books.

White, J. and Fadiman, J. (eds.) (1976) *Relax: How You Can Feel Better, Reduce Stress and Overcome Tension.* New York, NY: Confucian Press.

Williams, N. (2010) *Yoga Therapy for Every Special Child: Meeting Needs in a Natural Setting.* London: Singing Dragon/Jessica Kingsley Publishers.

Wilson, R.R. (1986) *Don't Panic: Taking Control of Anxiety Attacks.* New York, NY: Harper and Row.

Winston, D. and Maimes, S. (2007) *Adaptogens: Herbs for Strength, Stamina, and Stress Relief.* Rochester, VT: Healing Arts Press.

Yarema, T., Rhoda, D., and Branngen, J. (2006) *Eat, Taste, Heal: An Ayurvedic Cookbook for Modern Living.* Kapaa, HI: Five Elements Press.

Zemach-Bersin, D., Zemach-Bersin, K., and Reese, M. (1990) *Relaxercise: The Easy New Way to Health and Fitness.* San Francisco, CA: HarperCollins.

Subject Index

Author Index